Linguistic Fundamentals for Natural Language Processing

100 Essentials from Morphology and Syntax

Synthesis Lectures on Human Language Technologies

Editor
Graeme Hirst, *University of Toronto*

Synthesis Lectures on Human Language Technologies is edited by Graeme Hirst of the University of Toronto. The series consists of 50- to 150-page monographs on topics relating to natural language processing, computational linguistics, information retrieval, and spoken language understanding. Emphasis is on important new techniques, on new applications, and on topics that combine two or more HLT subfields.

Linguistic Fundamentals for Natural Language Processing: 100 Essentials from Morphology and Syntax
Emily M. Bender
2013

Semi-Supervised Learning and Domain Adaptation in Natural Language Processing
Anders Søgaard
2013

Semantic Relations Between Nominals
Vivi Nastase, Preslav Nakov, Diarmuid Ó Séaghdha, and Stan Szpakowicz
2013

Computational Modeling of Narrative
Inderjeet Mani
2012

Natural Language Processing for Historical Texts
Michael Piotrowski
2012

Sentiment Analysis and Opinion Mining
Bing Liu
2012

Discourse Processing
Manfred Stede
2011

Dependency Parsing
Sandra Kübler, Ryan McDonald, and Joakim Nivre
2009

Statistical Language Models for Information Retrieval
ChengXiang Zhai
2008

Linguistic Fundamentals for Natural Language Processing: 100 Essentials from Morphology and Syntax

Emily M. Bender

www.morganclaypool.com

ISBN: 9781627050111   paperback
ISBN: 9781627050128   ebook

DOI 10.2200/S00493ED1V01Y201303HLT020

A Publication in the Morgan & Claypool Publishers series
SYNTHESIS LECTURES ON HUMAN LANGUAGE TECHNOLOGIES

Lecture #20
Series Editor: Graeme Hirst, *University of Toronto*
Series ISSN
Synthesis Lectures on Human Language Technologies
Print 1947-4040   Electronic 1947-4059

Linguistic Fundamentals for Natural Language Processing

100 Essentials from Morphology and Syntax

Emily M. Bender
University of Washington

SYNTHESIS LECTURES ON HUMAN LANGUAGE TECHNOLOGIES #20

MORGAN & CLAYPOOL PUBLISHERS

ABSTRACT

Many NLP tasks have at their core a subtask of extracting the dependencies—who did what to whom—from natural language sentences. This task can be understood as the inverse of the problem solved in different ways by diverse human languages, namely, how to indicate the relationship between different parts of a sentence. Understanding how languages solve the problem can be extremely useful in both feature design and error analysis in the application of machine learning to NLP. Likewise, understanding cross-linguistic variation can be important for the design of MT systems and other multilingual applications. The purpose of this book is to present in a succinct and accessible fashion information about the morphological and syntactic structure of human languages that can be useful in creating more linguistically sophisticated, more language-independent, and thus more successful NLP systems.

KEYWORDS

NLP, morphology, syntax, linguistic typology, language variation

For Laurie Poulson

Contents

8   Argument types and grammatical functions

Acknowledgments

This book grew out of a tutorial I presented at the 2012 Conference of the North American Chapter of the Association for Computational Linguistics: Human Language Technologies, entitled "100 Things You Always Wanted to Know about Linguistics But Were Afraid to Ask*". I am grateful to Graeme Hirst for suggesting expanding that tutorial into a book. This book has also benefited from the thoughtful comments of Rebecca Dridan and two anonymous reviewers. Finally, I would like to thank the various people who answered my queries about the examples used in the text and other loose ends I was chasing down: Adam Albright, Sophia Ananiadou, Yoav Artzi, Tim Baldwin, Miriam Butt, Joshua Crowgey, Anita de Waard, Dan Flickinger, Antske Fokkens, Jeff Good, Varya Gracheva, Angelina Ivanova, Seppo Kittilä, Mayo Kudo, Thibaut Labarre, Peter Lippman, Lutz Marten, Steven Moran, Petya Osenova, Zina Pozen, Susanne Riehemann, Glenn Slayden, Lisa Tittle, Tom Wasow, Fei Xia, and Meliha Yetisgen-Yildiz.

Emily M. Bender
May 2013

*...for fear of being told 1000 more

CHAPTER 1

Introduction/motivation

#0 Knowing about linguistic structure is important for feature design and error analysis in NLP.

The field of linguistics includes subfields that concern themselves with different levels or aspects of the structure of language, as well as subfields dedicated to studying how linguistic structure interacts with human cognition and society. A sample of subfields is briefly described in Table 1.1. At each of those levels of linguistic structure, linguists find systematic patterns over enumerable units where both the units and the patterns have both similarities and differences across languages.

Table 1.1: A non-exhaustive sample of structural subfields of linguistics

Subfield	Description
Phonetics	The study of the sounds of human language
Phonology	The study of sound systems in human languages
Morphology	The study of the formation and internal structure of words
Syntax	The study of the formation and internal structure of sentences
Semantics	The study of the meaning of sentences
Pragmatics	The study of the way sentences with their semantic meanings are used for particular communicative goals

Machine learning approaches to NLP require features which can describe and generalize across particular instances of language use such that the machine learner can find correlations between language use and its target set of labels. It is thus beneficial to NLP that natural language strings have implicit structure and that the field of linguistics has been studying and elucidating that structure. It follows that knowledge about linguistic structures can inform the design of features for machine learning approaches to NLP. Put more strongly: knowledge of linguistic structure will lead to the design of better features for machine learning.

Conversely, knowledge of linguistic structure can also inform error analysis for NLP systems. Specifically, system errors should be checked for linguistic generalizations which can suggest kinds of linguistic knowledge to add to the system.[1] For example, if expletive pronouns (non-

---

[1]Such error analysis is an excellent opportunity for collaboration between NLP researchers and linguists.

referring pronouns, see #89) are tripping up a coreference resolution system, system performance might be improved by adding a step that detects such pronouns first.

The goal of this book is to present information about linguistic structures that is immediately relevant to the design of NLP systems, in a fashion approachable to NLP researchers with little or no background in linguistics. The focus of this book will be on morphology and syntax (collectively known as morphosyntax) as structures at this level can be particularly relevant to text-based NLP systems. Similar books could (and should) be written concerning phonetics/phonology and semantics/pragmatics. The reader is encouraged to approach the book with particular NLP tasks in mind, and ask, for each aspect of linguistic structure described here, how it could be useful to those tasks.

#1 Morphosyntax is the difference between a sentence and a bag of words.

Morphosyntax is especially relevant to text-based NLP because so many NLP tasks are related to or rely on solutions to the problem of extracting from natural language a representation of who did what to whom. For example: machine translation seeks to represent the same information (including, at its core, who did what to whom) given in the source language in the target language; information extraction and question answering rely on extracting relations between entities, where both the relations and the entities are expressed in words; sentiment analysis is interested in who feels what about whom (or what); etc.[2] To attempt these tasks by treating each sentence (or paragraph or document) as a bag of words is to miss out on a lot of information encoded in the sentence. Consider the contrasts in meaning between the following sets of sentences (from English and Japanese):[3]

(1) a. Kim sent Pat Chris.

 b. Kim sent Pat to Chris.

 c. Kim was sent to Pat by Chris.

 d. Kim was sent Pat by Chris.

---

[2]Even tasks that aren't concerned with the meaning expressed in the strings they process (e.g., the construction of language models) are impacted by morphosyntax in as much as they care about word order and/or identifying inflected forms as belonging to the same lemma.

[3]All examples from languages other than English in this book are presented in the format of interlinear glossed text (IGT), which consists of three or four lines: The first two lines represent the example in the source language, with one giving source language orthography and the second (optionally, for non-roman orthographies) a transliteration. At least one of these will indicate morpheme boundaries. The remaining two lines give a morpheme-by-morpheme gloss and a free translation into English. The morpheme-by-morpheme glosses use abbreviations for 'grams' (elements like PST for past tense). In general, these should conform to the Leipzig glossing rules [Bickel *et al.*, 2008], but may differ when the original source was using different conventions. The grams used in the IGT in this book are listed in Appendix A. When a gram is relevant to the discussion at hand, its meaning will be explained. The last line includes the ISO 639-3 language code indicating the language of the example.

(2) a. 田中　　が　ライオンを　食べた。
    Tanaka ga   raion   wo tabe-ta
    Tanaka NOM lion   ACC eat-PST

   'Tanaka ate the lion.' [jpn]

  b. 田中　　を　ライオンが　食べた。
    Tanaka wo raion   ga   tabe-ta
    Tanaka ACC lion   NOM eat-PST

   'The lion ate Tanaka.' [jpn]

  c. 田中　　が　ライオンに　食べられた。
    Tanaka ga   raion   ni   tabe-rare-ta
    Tanaka NOM lion   DAT eat-PASS-PST

   'Tanaka was eaten by the lion.' [jpn]

  d. 田中　　が　ライオンに　ケーキを　食べられた。
    Tanaka ga   raion   ni   keeki wo tabe-rare-ta
    Tanaka NOM lion   DAT cake   ACC eat-PASS-PST

   'The lion ate the cake (to Tanaka's detriment).' [jpn]

Conversely, ignoring morphosyntax can obscure the connection between strings which in fact mean the same thing or have closely related meanings. This can be illustrated with the set of examples in (3), which all involve the same fundamental 'giving' situation.

(3) a. Kim gave Sandy a book.

  b. Kim gave a book to Sandy.

  c. A book was given to Sandy by Kim.

  d. This is the book that Kim gave to Sandy.

  e. Which book do you think Kim gave to Sandy?

  f. It's a book that Kim gave to Sandy.

  g. This book is difficult to imagine that Kim could give to Sandy.

#2 The morphosyntax of a language is the constraints that it places on how words can be combined both in form and in the resulting meaning.

Formal linguists typically study morphosyntax from the point of view of grammaticality, describing sets of rules (or alternatively, sets of constraints) which delimit the set of grammatical sentences in a language. Thus pairs of examples like the following are interesting because they potentially illuminate rules (or constraints) that might not be apparent from more run-of-the-mill constructions:

(4) a. Which articles did John file __ without reading __?

b. *John filed a bunch of articles without reading __.

Example (4a) illustrates a phenomenon called 'parasitic gaps'.[4] The * indicates that (4b) is judged to be ungrammatical; __ indicates a position in the sentence where something is 'missing', compared to other related sentences.[5]

Other linguists, including typologists (linguists who study cross-linguistic variation), field linguists (linguists who do primary descriptive work on little-known languages), and grammar engineers (computational linguists who build machine readable hand-crafted grammars), also look at languages in terms of sets of rules or constraints, but tend to put more emphasis on how those constraints relate form to meaning.

For example, Nichols observes in her grammar of Ingush (a Nakh-Daghestanian language of the Caucasus) that "[t]he verb agrees with its nominative argument," and illustrates the point with several examples including the following (2011:432):[6]

(5) a. jett aara-b.ealar
       cow out-B.go.wp

       'The cow went out.' [inh]

b. zhwalii aara-d.ealar
       dog   out-D.go.wp

       'The dog went out.' [inh]

The difference in the verb forms between these two examples (*b* vs. *d*) reflects the noun class (or 'gender') of the subject. This can be seen as a constraint on well-formedness (if the verb doesn't agree with the gender of the noun bearing nominative case, the sentence is ill-formed) but also as a constraint on possible interpretations: If the verb does not agree with the noun, there may well be some other structure which could be assigned but not one in which the noun is functioning as the subject.

While the notion of grammaticality isn't always of interest in NLP (though it is useful in generation), the view of grammars as constraints on possible structures or possible relationships between words in given sentences is highly relevant.

---

[4]These examples and their judgments are from Engdahl 1983.

[5]While most syntactic theories make a binary distinction between grammatical and ungrammatical strings, human acceptability judgments are famously more gradient than that [Schütze, 1996, Ch. 3]. Linguists will sometimes use ?, ??, and ?* to indicate degrees of (un)acceptability between fully acceptable and fully unacceptable strings.

[6]wp stands for 'witnessed past tense', which contrasts in the tense system of Ingush with present, future and non-witnessed past forms. For explanation of the symbols used in glosses, see Appendix A.

#3 Languages use morphology and syntax to indicate who did what to whom, and make use of a range of strategies to do so.

Morphosyntax differentiates a sentence from a bag of words (see #1) by adding non-linear structure. That structure encodes information about the relationships between words. Individual words (specifically open class words) denote properties or situations. The structures (and function words) connecting those words build referring expressions out of properties and link the referring expressions to participant roles in the situations. This includes the bare-bones 'who did what to whom' as well as elaborations ("what kind of who did what kind of thing to what kind of whom, where, why, when and how").

Many of the topics covered in the 'syntax' sections of this book concern the various means that languages use for indicating that structure within the string. Linguists understand the structure in terms of multiple linked levels, including the surface form of words and their order, constituent structure, grammatical functions, and semantic predicate-argument structure. These various levels and their relevance to NLP will be discussed in Chapters 5–9.

In many languages, a lot of the information about sentence structure is reflected in the form of the words. The 'morphology' sections of this book concern the different kinds of information that can be expressed within a morphologically complex word (Chapters 2 and 4) and the relationship between the abstract morphological structure and its surface representation (Chapters 2–3).

In many NLP tasks, we want to extract from a sentence (as part of a text) precisely "who did what to whom" (and sometimes even "what kind of who did what kind of thing to what kind of whom, where, why, when and how"). Thus understanding how languages solve the inverse problem of encoding this information can help us more effectively design systems to extract it.

The subfield of linguistic typology is concerned with studying the range of variation across languages, both with an eye towards understanding the boundaries of that range (and thus universals of linguistic structure) as well as towards understanding the ways in which languages change over time and the various factors influencing those changes. Across all phenomena investigated by typologists, languages display interesting yet bounded variation. For example, to indicate 'who did what to whom', languages can and do use word order, case marking (differences in the form of the arguments), and agreement (differences in the form of the predicate), or a combination of those strategies, as described further in #78–80. The fact that languages vary in these ways, together with the fact that the range of variation is bounded, and in many cases, known, makes typology a very rich source of information for the design of NLP systems (see #6 and Bender 2011).

#4 Languages can be classified 'genetically', areally, or typologically.

Languages can be classified in several different ways. So called 'genetic' or 'genealogical' classifications group languages according to shared precursor languages. All languages change over time. When speakers of a language are separated into smaller groups (by geography or socioeconomic factors), that language change leads to divergence and eventually mutual incomprehensibility. A familiar example of this is the development of Latin into the Romance languages, including French, Italian, Spanish, Catalan, and Portuguese, as well as perhaps less familiar Romance languages such as Walloon, Romansch, and Piemontese. The Ethnologue [Lewis, 2009] lists 41 Romance languages in total. This same pattern of language genesis is happening worldwide. While it is easier to reconstruct where there exist written records of the ancestor language, the comparative method in historical linguistics [Meillet, 1925, Rankin, 2008] allows linguists to work from modern languages only to a time-depth of about 8,000 years [Nichols, 1992, 6] to 10,000 years [Rankin, 2008, 207]. The comparative method is predicated on similarities between the languages, both in lexicon and in grammar. Most relevant from the point of view of NLP is that languages will tend to share grammatical properties with other languages that they are related to through common descent.

A second type of classification of languages is 'areal', that is, based on the geographical area in which the languages are (or historically were) spoken. Areal classifications are important because one driver of language change is language contact: situations where speakers of one language interact with speakers of another language over extended periods time, either from positions of roughly equal power or in power asymmetries [Thomason and Kaufman, 1988]. Genealogical and areal classifications will partially overlap, as related languages tend to be spoken in geographically contiguous areas (but not necessarily), but not all areally related languages are also genealogically related.

A third type of classification is typological. Typological classifications categorize languages based on aspects of their grammar (e.g., the number of distinct vowel sounds contrasted or their strategy for indicating syntactic and semantic roles). While genetically or areally related languages are likely to share typological properties [Comrie, 1989, Ch. 10],[7] typological patterns, in both individual grammatical features and dependencies between them, recur across the world's languages [Daumé III and Campbell, 2007, Greenberg, 1963]. Thus, typological classifications can also join languages that are neither descended from a common ancestor nor spoken in close proximity to each other.

While all three classifications can in principle be multidimensional (see #5 below on why this is so for genetic classifications), it is most strongly true for typological classifications. That is, while some typological properties tend to pattern together (e.g., languages with verb-object word order are likely to have relative clauses which follow, rather than precede, nouns [Daumé III and Campbell, 2007, Greenberg, 1963]) such generalizations are rarely, if ever, absolute and at any rate only cover a small fraction of the possible combinations of typological properties.

---

[7]See also Daumé III 2009, Georgi et al. 2010.

#5 There are approximately 7,000 known living languages distributed across 128 language families.

The Ethnologue [Lewis, 2009], a reference work whose goal is to be a comprehensive catalog of all living languages, currently lists 6,909 languages distributed across 128 language families.[8] That number can change due to both language loss (as the last fully fluent speakers of endangered languages die) as well as additional linguistic field work, which can lead to descriptions of languages previously unknown to the field and/or reclassification of language varieties previously considered dialects of the same language into separate (but related) languages and vice versa. There are also cases of language genesis, perhaps the most famous recent example of which is the development of Nicaraguan Sign Language in schools for the deaf set up in the 1970s and 1980s and bringing together the deaf community in Nicaragua for the first time [Kegl *et al.*, 1999].

Another type of language genesis is the process of creolization [Thomason and Kaufman, 1988]. Pidgins arise in language contact situations (often involving slavery) where speakers of one or more 'substrate' languages must learn to use vocabulary from a 'superstrate' language to communicate with those in power. This results in a relatively impoverished language variety called a 'pidgin'. If children are exposed to the pidgin and acquire it as a native language, they elaborate it into a more rich linguistic system, called a 'creole'.[9] Creoles do not fit neatly into language family trees because their development represents breaks in continuity compared to other processes of language change, and because they develop out of multiple languages.

The Ethnologue lists 116 language families with more than one language, ranging in size from 2 languages (e.g., Left May, Papua New Guinea) to 1,532 (Niger-Congo). Indo-European, the family including most familiar European languages, is listed as including 439 languages, within 9 sub-families. In addition, the Ethnologue catalogs 73 languages which are still considered 'unclassified'; 56 language isolates (or families with just one language), including Basque; 82 creoles; 17 pidgins; 130 signed languages; and 1 constructed language (Esperanto).[10] Note that while these categories are all included in the language family index, they are not the same type of category. For example, while some signed languages are related to each other through common descent just as spoken languages are, they do not form one family.[11]

As mentioned in #4 above, language families are established and ancestor languages reconstructed through the comparative method [Meillet, 1925, Rankin, 2008]. The comparative method looks for shared vocabulary (and also shared grammatical structures) to determine whether any pair or set of languages are likely to be related to each other and for patterns of sound correspondences to establish possible sound changes and thus the forms of the ancestor language.

---

[8]www.ethnologue.com, accessed 7/13/12

[9]While there are several language varieties around the world with the terms 'pidgin' or 'creole' as part of their names, these uses do not necessarily align with the technical linguistic use of these terms.

[10]www.ethnologue.com, accessed 7/13/12

[11]The field has not achieved consensus on the classification of languages into families. In addition to the Ethnologue's classification, other major resources include Hammarström 2007, Moseley *et al.* 1994, Voegelin and Voegelin 1977; the WALS genealogical language list [Dryer, 2005] and Glottolog: `http://glottolog.livingsources.org` [Nordhoff *et al.*, 2011] .

Care must be taken to distinguish borrowing of words across languages from cognates descended from the same ancestor language root.

The boundaries between contact-induced language change and full-fledged creolization are not entirely clear. As such, a 'tree' model of language genealogy (where each language has just one parent) is somewhat problematic [McMahon and McMahon, 2003]. Nonetheless, linguists' classification of languages into language families can be a useful lens through which to view the languages of the world, or even just the languages that a particular NLP project is concerned with.

Most work in NLP to date has mainly focused on Indo-European languages, and only a small handful of those. Table 1.2 lists the most commonly studied languages in a survey of ACL 2008 and EACL 2009 papers, along with their language families and representative other languages from the same family. Table 1.3 lists the five most populous language families (again according to Ethnologue [Lewis, 2009]) with total number of languages, percentage of the world's population which can be counted among their speakers, and example languages. The relative dearth of NLP work on the vast majority of the world's languages casts doubt on the cross-linguistic applicability (or 'language-independence') of modern NLP techniques [Bender, 2011].

Table 1.2: Most commonly studied languages at recent conferences [Bender, 2011]

Language	Family	% ACL 2008	% EACL 2009	Other languages in family
English	Indo-European	63%	55%	French, Welsh, Gujarati
German	Indo-European	4%	7%	Latvian, Ukrainian, Farsi
Chinese	Sino-Tibetan	4%	2%	Burmese, Akha
Arabic	Afro-Asiatic	3%	1%	Hebrew, Somali, Coptic

#6 Incorporating information about linguistic structure and variation can make for more cross-linguistically portable NLP systems.

One of the advantages to machine learning approaches to NLP is that they can in principle be applied across languages. Where rule-based approaches typically require the development of rule sets specific to each language handled, machine learning algorithms only need data.[12] However, it does not follow that the best way to create a language-independent NLP system is to avoid coding in any linguistic knowledge. On the contrary, by treating textual input as simply a set of strings (or a bag of words) and not taking language on its own terms, we risk 'overfitting' to typological properties of a few well-studied (and in some cases, closely related) development languages.

This point is elaborated at length in Bender 2011. Here I will briefly summarize how linguistic knowledge can be incorporated into machine learning NLP systems to improve their cross-

---

[12]In the case of supervised machine learning, the data needs to be labeled, of course.

Table 1.3: Five most populous language families, from Ethnologue[13]

Language family	Living languages	Examples	% population
Indo-European	430	English Welsh Pashto Bengali	44.78
Sino-Tibetan	399	Mandarin Chinese Sherpa Burmese	22.28
Niger-Congo	1,495	Swahili Wolof Bissa	6.26
Afro-Asiatic	353	Arabic, Modern Standard Coptic Somali	5.93
Austronesian	1,246	Tagalog Balinese Hawaiian	5.45
Total	3,923		84.7

linguistic portability: (i) Understanding how languages vary can help researchers identify tacit assumptions about language structure that may hold true of the primary development languages, but not other languages of interest. For example, one way in which English differs from many languages is its relatively impoverished morphological system (few forms per lemma; few morphemes per word). Another (related) property specific to English is its relatively rigid word order. These properties surely affect the effectiveness of n-gram and bag-of-words approaches to tasks. (ii) Understanding how languages vary can help in the development of feature sets which accommodate a broader range of languages. For example, cheap approximations of morphology which define features looking at up to n characters at the end of the word could be generalized to handle prefixing languages (see #21) by also looking at the beginning of the word. Adding in extra features like this would presumably work best in combination with feature selection techniques that allow for automatic customization to particular languages. (iii) Finally, there are databases (notably WALS [Dryer and Haspelmath, 2011], see #100) which summarize typological properties of languages. Given that such information is available, and given that the set of natural languages is finite (subject to the relatively slow process of language change), it does not reduce the general-

[13]www.ethnologue.com/ethno_docs/distribution.asp; accessed on 2/6/09

ity of an NLP system to choose algorithms or feature sets based on typological properties which can be looked up.

The following chapters include examples from a wide range of languages. My purpose in doing so is to give the reader a sense of the rich variety of human languages. I hope that examples that seem particularly strange to readers most familiar with the languages commonly studied in NLP will prompt readers to consider how the performance of the systems they are working on would be affected by the differences between well-studied languages and the others considered here, and further how to generalize those systems in light of the cross-linguistic differences.

CHAPTER 2

Morphology: Introduction

#7 Morphemes are the smallest meaningful units of language, usually consisting of a sequence of phones paired with concrete meaning.

Morphology is the subfield of linguistics concerned with the formation and internal structure of words. It encompasses *morphotactics*, or questions of which morphemes are allowed to combine within a word and in what order; *morphophonology*, how the form of morphemes is conditioned by other morphemes they combine with; and *morphosyntax*, how the morphemes in a word affect its combinatoric potential.[1] In all three cases, the units under consideration are *morphemes*, which can be defined as the smallest meaningful units of language. A morpheme is typically a sequence of phones (sounds) paired with a concrete meaning.[2]

A simple example is given in (6) where the boundaries between morphemes (with words) are indicated by '+':

(6)   Morpheme+s are the small+est mean+ing+ful unit+s of language.

This example, however, belies the actual complexity of morphological systems. As described below, both the 'form' and the 'meaning' part of the pairing can vary from the prototypes in important ways. Specifically, the form can be made up of phones which are not contiguous (#8), it can be made up of something other than phones (#9), it can in fact be null (#10), and finally the form can vary with the linguistic context (#23–#26). On the meaning side, in addition to core lexical meaning (#11), morphemes can convey changes to that meaning (#12) (which furthermore can be idiosyncratic (#13)) and/or syntactically or semantically relevant features (#14, #28–#43)

#8 The phones making up a morpheme don't have to be contiguous.

While prototypical morphemes are sequences of phones (sounds, represented by letters in alphabetic writing systems) which furthermore have easily identified boundaries between them, there are several ways in which morphemes can depart from this prototypical case. The first is morphemes which consist of sequences of phones but are non-contiguous.

---

[1]Note that this is a different sense of the term 'morphosyntax' than is used in e.g., #1–#3.

[2]Some contemporary authors in morphological theory take issue with the concept of a morpheme, and develop theories that are instead based on notions of *paradigms* or *processes* [e.g., Anderson, 1992, Stump, 2001]. For the purposes of understanding how linguistic structure can be better leveraged in NLP systems, these theoretical issues are not immediately relevant.

The canonical example of such a morpheme comes from the so-called root and pattern morphology common in Semitic languages. An example from Hebrew [Arad, 2005, 27] is given in (7).

(7)

Root	Pattern	Part of Speech	Phonological Form	Orthographic Form	Gloss
ktb	CaCaC	(v)	katav	כתב	'wrote'
ktb	hiCCiC	(v)	hixtiv	הכתיב	'dictated'
ktb	miCCaC	(n)	mixtav	מכתב	'a letter'
ktb	CCaC	(n)	ktav	כתב	'writing, alphabet'

[heb]

(7) shows a range of forms built on the root *ktb*. The forms each involve the combination of the root with a different pattern. The patterns include slots for each of the consonants in the root as well as additional phonological material. The roots and patterns are identified through linguistic analysis and are identifiable because the same patterns recur with different roots. The actual forms also reflect morphophonological processes (see #24), such that the surface phone corresponding to the root's *k* is sometimes *x*, and the surface phone corresponding to the root's *b* is *v*.[3]

Another way in which morphemes can end up as non-contiguous sequences of phones is through the process of infixation. (8) gives a set of examples from Lakhota [Albright, 2000], illustrating the variable position of the morpheme *-wa-*, which indicates agreement with a first person singular subject ('I').[4] For present purposes, what is important is that in the infixed forms, the *-wa-* morpheme interrupts the root, rendering the root non-contiguous.

(8) Prefixed:

lówan	'he sings'	wa-lówan	'I sing'
núwe	'he swims'	wa-núwe	'I swim'
káge	'he does/makes'	wa-káge	'I do/make'

Infixed:

m'ani	'he walks'	ma-wá-ni	'I walk'
aphé	'he hits'	a-wá-phe	'I hit'
hoxpé	'he coughs'	ho-wá-xpe	'I cough'

[lkt]

---

[3]This is a phonological representation of Hebrew, rather than a transliteration of the standard written form. The standard written form typically does not represent the vowels.
[4]On person and number, see #30; on agreement, see #38.

#9 The form of a morpheme doesn't have to consist of phones.

While morphemes prototypically consist of one or more phones (perhaps with associated stress or tone marking), they don't have to. One obvious example is morphemes in signed languages, in which the minimal units of form include parameters like handshape, hand location, hand orientation and trajectory [Brentari, 1998]. Examples can also be found from spoken languages. A case in point are morphemes consisting solely of changes to the tone pattern of a word. Tonal languages associate syllables with relative pitch values (or pitch change patterns), and these pitch distinctions can be contrastive, making the difference between words.

(9) (from Noonan 1992:92) provides a set of examples from Lango (a Nilo-Saharan language of Uganda). These examples are all different inflected forms of the verb 'to stop'. They all agree with a first person singular subject ('I'), but differ in their aspect.[5] The only difference between the first two forms is in the tone associated with the final syllable. In the perfective form (indicating completed action) the syllable is associated with a low tone. In the habitual form it bears a falling (high to low) tone.

(9)

Form	Gloss
àgíkò	'I stop (something), perfective'
àgíkô	'I stop (something), habitual'
àgíkkò	'I stop (something), progressive'

[laj]

#10 The form of a morpheme can be null.

The previous two vignettes describe cases where morphemes consist of something other than contiguous sequences of phones, but in all cases discussed so far, there is at least some phonological material[6] to constitute the form part of the form-meaning pair. Even this does not need to be the case: There are plenty of morphemes which are zero in form. Their presence is nonetheless detectable because they stand in contrast to non-zero forms in the same position in the word.

The singular forms of count nouns in English provide one example: *cat* (singular) contrasts with *cats* (plural). It may be tempting to analyze this instead in terms of count nouns being fundamentally singular (so that *cat* involves just one morpheme). This would require positing a rule of morphology that add the *-s* and changes the number from singular to plural. Such an analysis still leaves a morphological analyzer with the problem of knowing to posit singular number just in case there is not an overt mark of plural.[7]

Another example comes from French verbal inflection (focusing here on the orthographic form rather than the pronunciation; the pronunciation has even more zeroes). The table in (10)

---

[5]On aspect, see #29.
[6]Here I am using this term to also apply to the minimal units of form in signed languages.
[7]While it is not uncommon for singular number to be the 'null' in a number paradigm, some languages do have overt marking of both singular and plural number, for example Italian *gatto* 'cat' v. *gatti* 'cats'.

shows the present tense paradigm for the verb *manger* 'to eat', for which the root is *mange*. The cells for first and third person singular ('I' and 'he/she/it') take forms of the verb identical to the root. This is analyzed as a zero morpheme which is ambiguous between first person singular and third person singular (or alternatively, two zero morphemes).

(10)

	SG		PL	
1	je mange	'I eat'	nous mangeons	'we eat'
2	tu manges	'you (sg) eat'	vous mangez	'you (pl) eat'
3	il/elle mange	'he/she/it eats'	ils/elles mangent	'they eat'

[fra]

Another case where the effects of the type that can be associated with an overt morpheme can also be associated with null morphemes (or zeroes) is found in processes by which a word of one part of speech can be used as another, without any overt mark of the change. English has many many roots which can be either nouns or verbs, including cases where the meanings are closely related, arguing for a morphological relationship rather than accidental homophony. Examples include *slide*, *storm*, and *switch*. With some newer forms, it's relatively easy to see which use came first: *Google* the noun (referring to the search engine) surely preceded *Google* the verb ('to perform a search using Google'). This kind of morphological process is an example of derivational morphology (see #12 below). Accordingly, it is often called 'zero derivation'. Here it is not the contrast to other morphemes in the same position but the change in behavior of the overall form which indicates the presence of the zero.

Zero morphemes are relevant to computational applications because of their impact on morphological analyzers. The task of a morphological analyzer is to recover the information added by inflectional morphemes such as these (see #28ff below) and so it must be able to detect zero morphemes as well as overt ones. Fortunately, there is enough information in the system of contrasts that this is possible in principle.

#11 Root morphemes convey core lexical meaning.

In the canonical case, a word consists of one *root* morpheme and zero or more affixes.[8] The root morpheme conveys the core lexical meaning of the word. Some examples from English and Turkish are given in (11), the roots underlined and morphemes separated by -:[9]

(11)   a. <u>cat</u>

     b. <u>jump</u>-ing

     c. <u>amaze</u>-ment

---

[8]A *root* is always monomorphemic. A *stem* is a root or a combination of a root and one or more affixes that can take yet more affixes.

[9](11) glosses *cat* as monomorphemic. While this is true at least in the sense that all of the phones in the form are assigned to the root morpheme, many analyses of English morphology would identify a second morpheme (whose form is the empty string) marking singular number, see #10.

d. de-<u>act</u>-iv-ate

e. <u>dayan</u>-a-m-ıyor-um
    bear-PSB-NEG-IMPF-1SG

'(I) can't bear (it).' [tur] [Göksel and Kerslake, 2005, 406]

While in the canonical case there is just one root morpheme per word, this generalization, too, has exceptions. The most common one is compounding, which is speculated to be common to all languages (or nearly so; Guevara and Scalise 2009). Compounding straddles the boundary between morphology and syntax, behaving in some ways like word-formation and in others like phrase-formation, but to the extent that it is morphological, it provides plenty of examples of words containing more than one root. This is illustrated by the following examples of compounds from English, German and Mandarin:[10]

(12) a. celestial sphere

    b. beam-width

    c. sunset

    d. Himmelshälfte
      Himmel-s-hälfte
      heaven-LNK-half

      'half the sky' [deu]

    e. 天球
      tiān qiú
      sky   ball

      'celestial sphere' [cmn]

Compounding is also recursive, allowing compound words to be compounded into still longer words. Some examples, again from English, German and Mandarin:

(13) a. airline reservation counter

    b. Rettungshubschraubernotlandeplatz
      Rettung-s-hubschrauber-not-lande-platz
      rescue-LNK-helicopter-emergency-landing-place

      'Rescue helicopter emergency landing pad' [deu]

    c. 中國語新字典
      zhōng   guó   yǔ   xīn zì   diǎn
      middle   kingdom language new character scholarship

      'New Chinese Language Dictionary' [cmn] [Starosta *et al.*, 1997, 355]

[10]English has many compounds written with a space or a hyphen, as well as those written as one contiguous form. German tends to write compounds without spaces, and furthermore has linking morphemes (LNK in (12d) and (13b)) connecting the roots, see Goldsmith and Reutter 1998.

Another, less common, exception to the one-root-per-word generalization is noun incorporation [Mithun, 1984]. In noun incorporation, a noun stem is included in the affixes to a verbal root. The noun stem typically provides information about one of the arguments to a verb, though doesn't necessarily fill that argument position. That is, in some noun incorporation constructions, there can be a separate noun phrase in the sentence in addition to the incorporated noun stem. (14) gives and example from Gunwinggu (an Australian language):[11]

(14)   … bene-<u>dulg</u>-<u>naŋ</u>   mangaralaljmayn.
          they.DU-tree-saw cashew.nut

'…They saw a cashew tree.' [gup]

Note also that there are some monomorphemic words (words consisting only of a root morpheme) which arguably don't mean anything. These are the syntactic function words discussed in #88 and expletive pronouns discussed in #89.

#12 Derivational affixes can change lexical meaning.

Linguists draw a distinction between two types of affixes: derivational affixes and inflectional affixes [Anderson, 2006]. As with many linguistic classifications, the boundary between these two categories is not always clear (*Ibid.*). Broadly speaking, however, derivational affixes can change the part of speech (see #47), argument structure (see #54) or meaning of the stem they combine with. Inflectional affixes (see #14), on the other hand, typically provide syntactically or semantically relevant features, without changing information already present in the stem.

Table 2.1 (adapted from O'Grady *et al.* 2010:124) presents a sample of English derivational affixes. Where English is relatively impoverished when it comes to inflectional morphology, it has a large inventory of derivational affixes. As illustrated in Table 2.1, many but not all of these change the part of speech of the resulting form. Even those that don't change the part of speech still change the meaning (such that *king* and *kingdom* stand in a regular semantic relationship to each other, but do not mean the same thing).

When linguists identify a part of a word as a derivational affix, they are making the analytical claim that that affix has (or had, at some prior point in the development of the language) the ability to attach productively to any stem of some appropriately defined class. However, as with all other parts of a language, morphological systems can change over time. Existing affixes can lose their productivity and new productive affixes can enter the language, such as *-gate* 'scandal' in English [Lehrer, 1988]. When a derivational affix loses its productivity, however, it doesn't immediately disappear from the language, but rather persists in a set of forms until further language change causes enough of those words to become archaic (cease to be used) or change their pronunciation enough that the affix is no longer identifiable. The upshot for automatic processing of language is that in derivational morphology (as in many other linguistic subsystems) there will be many patterns of varying generality [Brinton and Traugott, 2005].

---

[11]Example from Oates 1964 cited in Mithun 1984:867.

Table 2.1: A sample of English derivational affixes [O'Grady *et al.*, 2010, 124]

Affix	POS change	Examples
-able	V → A	fixable, doable, understandable
-ive	V → A	assertive, impressive, restrictive
-al	V → N	refusal, disposal, recital
-er	V → N	teacher, worker
-ment	V → N	adjournment, treatment, amazement
-dom	N → N	kingdom, fiefdom
-less	N → A	penniless, brainless
-ic	N → A	cubic, optimistic
-ize	N → V	hospitalize, vaporize
-ize	A → V	modernize, nationalize
-ness	A → N	happiness, sadness
anti-	N → N	antihero, antidepressant
de-	V → V	deactivate, demystify
un-	V → V	untie, unlock, undo
un-	A → A	unhappy, unfair, unintelligent

#13 Root+derivational affix combinations can have idiosyncratic meanings.

Derivational affixes can persist in words even after they have lost their generality because of the process of lexicalization: In addition to manipulating productive processes, speakers of languages also internalize the results of those processes, at least for certain sufficiently frequent forms [Alegre and Gordon, 1999, Brinton and Traugott, 2005]. Once a root+derivational affix form has become part of the stored lexicon of (speakers of) a language, it is potentially subject to the processes of semantic change that potentially affect all words. In addition, some forms are deliberately coined with a specific referent in mind, and so may be somewhat non-compositional from the start. (15) gives some examples from English:

(15)   a. reality (real + ity)

     b. responsible (response + ible)

     c. transmission (transmit + tion)

One and the same derivational affix can be associated with both compositional (productive) and non-compositional (semantically drifted) forms. This means that any system attempting to automatically analyze derivational morphology is faced with some additional ambiguity resolution, to sift out the genuine (productive) uses from those to which the same meaning-change rules should not be applied. Note also that there can be single words with both idiosyncratic and compositional meanings: *transmission* as a part of a car is means more than *transmit + tion*, whereas in the sense of 'something which is sent' or 'the sending of something' its meaning is still very transparent.

#14 Inflectional affixes add syntactically or semantically relevant features.

Where root morphemes provide core lexical meaning and derivational affixes (often) add to that meaning, inflectional affixes add information which ranges from that which is at least semantically relevant to that which doesn't look like meaning at all. #29–#37 provide details about a wide range of syntactic and semantically relevant features which are marked morphologically in at least some languages. While English has a relatively rich collection of derivational affixes (see #12 above), it is notoriously sparse in inflectional morphology. O'Grady *et al.* [2010, 132] identify the affixes in Table 2.2 as an exhaustive list of English inflectional affixes.

Table 2.2: English inflectional affixes, adapted from O'Grady *et al.* 2010:132

Affix	Syntactic/semantic effect	Examples
-s	NUMBER: plural	*cats*
-'s	possessive	*cat's*
-s	TENSE: present, SUBJ: 3sg	*jumps*
-ed	TENSE: past	*jumped*
-ed/-en	ASPECT: perfective	*eaten*
-ing	ASPECT: progressive	*jumping*
-er	comparative	*smaller*
-est	superlative	*smallest*

Other linguists might take issue with this as an exhaustive list of inflectional morphemes. For one thing, it does not include the zero affixes which contrast with plural -*s* on nouns and 3rd person singular present tense -*s* on verbs, nor the zero affix which produces the base form of the verb that appears after the infinitival *to*. Another issue involves the possessive form, which has been argued (e.g., in Sag *et al.* 2003) to be a clitic (see #19) and not an affix. Conversely, the negative form -*n't* as in *didn't*, which many take to be a clitic, has been argued to be an affix [Zwicky and Pullum, 1983] (see #16).

No analysis of English inflectional morphology would claim that it has a rich inflectional system, however. Many other languages do. The inflectional system of English provides a small range of examples of the kind of syntactico-semantic features which inflectional affixes can contribute: number information (singular versus plural) on nouns, tense and aspect information on verbs, agreement between verbs and nouns, negation (on verbs) and comparative/superlative forms of adjectives. All of this information is semantically relevant. However, if we include the zero affix that makes the base form of the verb (after *to* in *to jump*, for example), then English inflectional morphology also serves to illustrate morphological marking of features with purely syntactic effects. In building cross-linguistically portable NLP systems, however, it is necessary to anticipate a broader range of information potentially marked in the morphology; see #29–#37 for an overview.

#15 Morphemes can be ambiguous and/or underspecified in their meaning.

Another type of complexity to the form-meaning relationship is ambiguity: one form with with multiple meanings. We see this across all types of morphemes. Ambiguity of root morphemes is ordinary lexical ambiguity, such that the form *bank* can be the financial institution, land alongside a river, or any one of a number of other senses.[12]

The English prefix *un-* provides an example of ambiguity in derivational morphemes. It can attach to either adjectives (*unsuitable*) or verbs (*undo*). In attaching to adjectives, its meaning is something like 'opposite', while attaching to verbs its meaning has to do with reversing the action named by the verb [Marchand, 1969, Maynor, 1979]. While this ambiguity is resolved by the part of speech of the stem, note that that is not always unambiguous itself. A case in point is the form *untieable* which, depending on the order of attachment of the prefix *un-* and the suffix *-able* involves either the adjective-attaching *un-* or the verb-attaching one.

Inflectional affixes also show ambiguity, even in the tiny sample provided by English. The form *-s* is used to mark both plural on nouns and present tense on verbs (specifically, verbs with third person singular subjects). This ambiguity interacts with the widespread part of speech ambiguity in English open class forms to give rise to forms like *slides* which could either be a plural noun or a third person singular present tense verb. Especially in cases of ambiguous inflectional affixes, the best analysis can be in terms of underspecification. A case in point is the zero which contrasts with *-s* in English present tense verb forms. This null morpheme marks present tense and any combination of person and number on the subject other than third person and singular. Rather than treating the remaining five person/number combinations in terms of five (or even two, one for plural, one for the singulars) zero affixes, it can be more efficient to posit one (null) affix which is underspecified between the five possible values [see Flickinger 2000].

Finally, note that ambiguities can span the border (fuzzy as it is) between inflectional and derivational morphology. The morphological marker of passivization in English is formally identical to the affix marking the past participle, that is *-en* or *-ed* or other irregular forms, depending on the verb, but always identical if the passive is available at all [Huddleston and Pullum, 2002, 77–78]. As a marker of aspectual information, the past participle affix falls squarely into the inflectional camp. The passive, however, brings with it effects on both the expected syntactic arguments and their linking to semantic arguments (see #84), and so is arguably a derivational affix.

[12]WordNet [Fellbaum, 1998], accessed online 7/17/12, lists 10 noun senses and 8 verb senses.

#16 The notion 'word' can be contentious in many languages.

The preceding discussion, like much work in linguistics and NLP, has assumed that the notion 'word' is unproblematic, and that given an utterance from any natural language, its segmentation into words would be uncontroversial. Unfortunately, this is not the case.

The issue of word segmentation is an immediate practical problem for languages whose orthographies do not use white space between words (or for that matter, anywhere within sentences), or do not do so reliably. Chinese, Japanese and Thai all fall into this category. The morphological analyzer ChaSen [Asahara and Matsumoto, 2000], which does tokenization, part of speech tagging and morphological analysis/tagging, segments off all elements which might be considered inflectional affixes in Japanese. Chinese has even less in the way of inflectional affixes than English does (arguably none), and so it would seem to present fewer problems. However, there are still plenty of multi-syllabic (and generally multimorphemic) words in Chinese (largely compounds) and so for Chinese, as well, the segmentation problem and even the intended target (gold-standard) are non-trivial [see, e.g., Xue, 2001].

For languages with a convention of using white space between words in the standard orthography, white space can be used as an approximation of word boundaries. However, even when the orthographic tradition provides white space, it isn't always a good guide to word boundaries from a linguistic point of view. One case in point here are the so-called clitics in Romance languages. Linguists have argued that the pre-verbal clitics (representing pronouns and negation, inter alia) actually belong to the same word as the verb they are attached to, in both French [Miller, 1992] and Italian [Monachesi, 1993]. An example from French (in standard orthography) is shown in (16):

(16) Je   ne te   le   donne pas.
      1SG.SBJ NEG 2SG.IOBJ 3SG.DOBJ give   NEG

      'I do not give it to you.' [fra]

Miller's arguments for treating the so-called clitics as affixes include the following: (i) they are selective about what they can attach to (verbs), (ii) not all predicted sequences of 'clitics' are possible, (iii) the 'clitics' are subject to morphophonological changes that are not expected across word boundaries, and (iv) the ordering of the 'clitics' is fixed and idiosyncratic. All of these properties are typical of word-internal systems and not typical of syntactic combinations. Furthermore, the interaction with coordination shows that the 'clitics' must attach low (to the lexical verb).

Finally, even in English, the tokenization of sentences into words is not completely clear-cut. One case in point is the negative marker *n't*. Because of the alternation with *not* shown in (17), it is tempting to view *n't* as an independent word, namely a reduced form of *not*:

(17)   a. Kim did not leave.

       b. Kim didn't leave.

This kind of reasoning is likely behind the decision of the creators of the Penn Treebank [Marcus *et al.*, 1993] to segment off *n't* into its own token. However, as argued in detail by Zwicky and Pullum [1983], the linguistic facts show that *didn't* and similar forms are single words. The sources of evidence or this conclusion are similar to those cited above for French,[13] including phonological idiosyncrasies such as the pronunciation (and spelling) of *won't*, which surely isn't pronounced like *willn't*.

#17 Constraints on order operate differently between words than they do between morphemes.

The question of where to draw word boundaries and whether particular morphemes are independent words or affixes belonging to a larger word may seem like the kind of theoretical issue which is of interest to linguists but does not have any practical implications for NLP. While there certainly are theoretical issues that meet that description, the question of word boundaries is not one of them. At the very least there is the practical problem of establishing gold standards for tokenization in light of linguistic uncertainty. Beyond that, there is the fact that the status of a morpheme as an affix or as an independent word has implications for its distribution in language.

Specifically, while the order of words is constrained (to varying degrees based on the language and the type of word) by the rules of syntax, words can generally be separated from the other words they are ordered with respect to by modifiers. For example, determiners precede nouns in English, but adjectives can intervene:

(18) a. The dog slept.

 b. The brown dog slept.

 c. The lazy, brown dog slept.

 d. The extremely lazy, yet rather ferocious, chocolate brown dog slept.

Affixes, on the other hand, are subject to much stricter sequencing constraints. It is typically possible to describe even complex morphological systems in terms of 'templates' with 'slots' each of which can be filled by exactly one morpheme at a time [Good, 2011, Sec. 2.3].[14] While any given slot can be optional, the overall systems tend to be much more rigid than what one finds in syntax. (19) from Hoijer 1971, 125 schematizes the prefix chain common to Athabaskan languages:

---

[13]Zwicky and Pullum [1983] in fact use the case of *n't* to illustrate their tests for distinguishing clitics from affixes; these tests are among those Miller applied to the French data.

[14]That morphological systems can be described in this way does not mean that this is the most linguistically adequate analysis; in particular, templates obscure any hierarchical relations among morphemes within a word [Good, 2011, Simpson and Withgott, 1986]. This point is orthogonal to the considerations at hand here, however.

(19)   1.   Zero or more adverbial prefixes
       2.   Prefix for the iterative paradigm
       3.   Pluralizing prefix
       4.   Object pronoun prefix
       5.   Deictic subject prefix
       6.   Zero, one or two adverbial prefixes
       7.   Prefix marking mode, tense or aspect
       8.   Subject pronoun prefix
       9.   Classifier prefix
       10. Stem

Because the distribution of independent words and affixes differ in this way, NLP systems can likely be improved designing different features capturing word ordering (and optionality) from those for affix ordering (and optionality) and by recognizing that white space may not be an unfailable indicator of independent word status.

#18 The distinction between words and morphemes is blurred by processes of language change.

Part of the reason that it can be difficult to determine whether a given morpheme is an independent word or a bound affix (i.e., a morpheme that can only appear as part of another word) is that as languages change morphemes can in fact move from being one to being the other. More specifically, a common type of language change follows what Hopper and Traugott [2003, 7] term the 'cline of grammaticality':

(20)   content item > grammatical word > clitic > inflectional affix

That is, over time, a word that was originally an independent word with rich lexical meaning (like *back* or *go*) acquires a grammatical use in which its meaning shifts and/or is bleached (e.g., *going to/gonna* as a marker of near future). At this point, the form is a grammatical word. The grammatical word use may gain stricter constraints on its distribution (e.g., must appear directly before a verb). The next point along this cline is 'clitic' (described in more detail in #19 below). Clitics are pronounced as part of an adjacent word even though they are still syntactically independent. From there, the next step is for the clitic to become an (inflectional) affix which is part of a larger word both phonologically and morphologically.[15]

Language change is not an orderly process, of course, but is rather characterized by variation: older and newer forms will co-exist, even within the speech (and writing) of individual speakers [Labov, 1982]. Thus when English developed *be going to* and *gonna*, it didn't lose the lexical verb *go*. At any given point in the language, there will be clear cut cases of affixes and

---

[15]This process doesn't leave us with ever longer inflectional chains because inflectional affixes can also be lost all together due to sound change.

independent words, but potentially also both ambiguous forms and forms which are simply hard to categorize. Fortunately for NLP, the exact classification of forms often might not matter: It should be sufficient to design feature sets (and systems) which anticipate the existence of all points along the cline in (20) and allow for ambiguity.

#19 A clitic is a linguistic element which is syntactically independent but phonologically dependent.

As mentioned above, *clitics* are morphemes that are intermediate between independent words and affixes. More specifically, clitics are syntactically independent (it is the rules of syntax which determine their location in the string) but phonologically dependent: they are not pronounced as their own words, but rather form a word together with something to the left or to the right. (Any given clitic will have a direction it 'leans' to find a host.)

As noted in #16 above, writing systems often do not provide reliable cues as to the status of clitics. An example of a clitic in English is the possessive marker *'s* as illustrated in the following examples from Sag *et al.* 2003, 199 (see also Zwicky 1982).

(21)   a. Jesse met the president of the university's cousin.

     b. Don't touch that plant growing by the trail's leaves.

     c. The person you were talking to's pants are torn.

The point of these examples is that the *'s* attaches not to the noun understood to be the possessor (*president*, *plant*, and *person*, respectively) but to the right edge of the noun phrase. Its distribution can be neatly described in terms of syntax (it takes an NP to its left and forms a constituent with that NP which can serve as a determiner for a larger NP). Phonologically, however, it is part of the word immediately to its left.

Zwicky [1982] describes a class of words called *leaners*, which includes clitics, but also other words which are phonologically dependent in the sense of forming a unit with a neighboring word and not bearing stress, but which don't quite form a word-like unit with their neighbor. In this class he includes English articles *a, an, the*, coordinating conjunctions, subject and object pronouns, and others.

In addition to clitics which seem to be positioned by more-or-less ordinary rules of syntax, there are also clitics which have a characteristic position within the string all their own. This position is usually the second position — after either the first word of a clause or the first constituent — and the phenomenon is characteristic of Slavic languages but not only found there [Anderson, 1993, Browne, 1974]. (22) (from Browne 1974, 41) is an example from Serbo-Croatian,[16]

---

[16]Serbo-Croatian, also called Bosnian-Croatian-Serbian (BCS), is a macro-language or family of closely related yet distinguishable language varieties. Browne [1974] cites these examples as coming from the Novi Sad and Belgrade areas, which indicates that they belong to the Ekavian variety of Serbo-Croatian, and could have been written with Latin or Cyrillic orthography at the time the data was collected. This example serves to highlight the difficulties in defining the notion 'language' (as opposed to 'dialect') and the importance of tracking which language variety any given piece of data represents.

which allows clitics to appear after either the first word or after the first constituent. (The clitics are underlined.)

(22) a. Taj <u>mi</u> <u>je</u> pesnik napisao knjigu.
          that I.SG PST poet   write   book

          'That poet wrote me a book.' [hbs]

      b. Taj pesnik <u>mi</u> <u>je</u> napisao knjigu.
          that poet   I.SG PST write   book

          'That poet wrote me a book.' [hbs]

#20 Languages vary in how many morphemes they have per word (on average and maximally).

One important way in which languages vary (and can be classified typologically, see #4) is in the number of morphemes they pack into each word. On one extreme are languages in which (nearly) every word consists of only one morpheme. The languages are called 'isolating' or 'analytic' languages. At the other end of the spectrum are 'synthetic' languages, which adorn words (especially verbs and/or nouns) with many affixes.

One way to conceive of the position of a language on this spectrum is in terms of its grammatical system, specifically, in terms of the longest words it has the potential to create. Oflazer [1996, 80] illustrates the morphological complexity of Turkish with the following (probably contrived) example:[17]

(23) uygar   +laş   +tır   +ama +yabil +ecek   +ler +imiz   +den
      civilized +AToV +CAUS +NEG +POT +VToA(AToN) +3PL +POSS.1PL +ABL(+NToV)

      +miş +siniz +cesine
      +PST +2PL +VToAdv

      '(behaving) as if you were one of those whom we might not be able to civilize' [tur]

However, a more typical way to explore this dimension is by counting words and morphemes in actual running text. Greenberg [1960] proposed an 'index of synthesis' which was simply the number of morphemes in some sample of text divided by the number of words. Karlsson [1998] presents the values for the index of synthesis for a sample of languages shown in Table 2.3.

Unfortunately, calculating the index of synthesis is quite labor intensive and requires detailed knowledge of the languages in question—and is not possible to calculate automatically without high quality morphological analyzers for each language. Wälchli [2012] developed an alternative method to measure degree of synthesis indirectly (and automatically), by comparing

---

[17]This example consists of just one word; the spaces have been inserted to improve the alignment between the morphemes and their glosses.

Table 2.3: Index of Synthesis values, from Karlsson 1998

Language	Index of synthesis
Vietnamese	1.06
Yoruba	1.09
English	1.68
Old English	2.12
Swahili	2.55
Turkish	2.86
Russian	3.33
Inuit (Eskimo)	3.72

the type-token ratio across languages over the same text.[18] He applies this metric to translations of passages from the Bible into 168 languages from 46 language families and observes that most of the samples "strive toward a medium degree of synthesis while highly synthetic and analytic languages are the exception." (p. 74)

In this calculation, English is situated towards the analytic end of the scale, without being one of the outliers. What this means for NLP is that most languages are more highly synthetic than English is, and that the cross-linguistic portability of NLP systems can in general be improved by anticipating more morphological complexity than is provided by English. In particular, it is important to anticipate morphological systems with multiple affixes on either side of the root (where English rarely has more than one, at least if we restrict our attention to inflectional morphology).

#21 Languages vary in whether they are primarily prefixing or suffixing in their morphology.

In addition to varying in terms of how many possible affixes a word can have and how many a typical word has, languages also vary in the position of the affixes within the word. In particular, with very few exceptions, affixes have a slot that they belong to within a word. Any given affix will be a prefix (appearing in the string of affix slots before the root), a suffix (appearing the string of affix slots after the root), or more rarely an infix (appearing within the root itself, see #8) or a circumfix (consisting of two parts, one before and one after the root). Languages differ in terms of how many of each type of affix they have.

Dryer [2011f] surveyed 971 languages, looking for the position of 10 specific different kinds of affixes (including case affixes on nouns, tense and aspect affixes on verbs, and others, all on nouns or verbs).[19] He then developed an index (giving more weight to certain types of affixes)

---

[18]As Wälchli points out, artifacts of orthography and translation introduce some noise into this measurement.

[19]This specifically concerns inflectional morphology, and not derivational morphology, in contrast to Wälchli's work cited in #20 above.

to calculate both how much affixation there is in general and what percentage of it is suffixes v. prefixes. The results are shown in Table 2.4.

Table 2.4: Prefixing vs. Suffixing in Inflectional Morphology from Dryer 2011f

Type	N Languages
Little or no inflectional morphology	141
Predominantly suffixing	406
Moderate preference for suffixing	124
Approximately equal amounts of suffixing and prefixing	147
Moderate preference for prefixing	94
Predominantly prefixing	59
Total	971

Note that English comes out as 'predominantly suffixing' on this scale, meaning that of the inflectional morphology it has (which is furthermore enough to avoid the 'little or no inflectional morphology' category), more than 80% of it appears after the root. Here English does fall into the majority category, but it is worth noting that a significant minority of the languages sampled (30%) fall into the prefixing categories and/or the equal preference category. Thus NLP systems that attempt to approximate morphology by looking at sequences of characters at the end of each word would be hampered by this assumption in roughly a third of the world's languages.

#22 Languages vary in how easy it is to find the boundaries between morphemes within a word.

Yet another dimension on which languages can vary in terms of their morphology is the degree to which morpheme boundaries are clearly identifiable. Languages with clear morpheme boundaries are *agglutinating* while those with morphologically complex forms that nonetheless aren't easily broken down into prefix*+root+suffix* sequences are called *fusional*. Turkish is an example of an agglutinating language. In the example in (24), while there may be multiple possible morphological analyses of the form, given a particular analysis there it is clear where the morpheme boundaries should be inserted.[20]

(24)   dayanamıyorum
       dayan-a-m-ıyor-um
       bear-PSB-NEG-IMPF-1SG

     '(I) can't bear (it).' [tur] [Göksel and Kerslake, 2005, 406]

Such cases of clear morpheme boundaries contrast with cases which are murkier because of complex phonological processes (see #23–#26) or because the morphemes involved don't take the

---

[20]Both the range of possible analyses and the morpheme boundaries on any given analysis are established by comparing many Turkish words to each other.

form of sequences of phones at all, as with the Semitic root and pattern morphology described in #8, tonal morphemes as discussed in #9, and also stem changes such as is found in English irregular past tense verbs (*sang* < *sing* + past).

Bickel and Nichols [2011b] survey the expression of case and tense/aspect/mood in 165 languages to determine whether they were expressed with purely concatenative morphology (including possibly obscure phonological changes), tone changes, or 'ablaut' (changes internal to the stem, including the Semitic systems (#8)). In all, they found 6 languages in their sample that used tonal morphemes for case and/or tense/aspect/mood and 5 which used ablaut. Given the degree of complexity of the phonological processes that can obscure morpheme boundaries and the fact that they were looking at regular patterns (and not irregular forms, like the *sang* example above which tend to have high token frequency), this probably underestimates the potential for unclear morpheme boundaries to present problems for NLP systems.

A closely related property is the extent to which single morphemes express multiple morphosyntactic features. For example, the English plural marker *-s* on nouns expresses only plural number. On the other hand, the affix *-s* which attaches to verbs expresses both agreement with the subject (third person singular) and tense (present). There is no way to divide that *-s* up into the part that means 'present tense' and the part that means 'third person singular subject'.

Bickel and Nichols [2011a] term this property 'exponence' and investigate it in a sample of 162 languages, looking particularly at morphemes that express case and those that express tense/aspect/mood (where tense/aspect/mood is taken as one category, not three), and then asking whether they also express anything else. In their sample, they found that monoexponence—affixes expressing just one morphosyntactic property—was by far the norm (71/87 languages with case markers used those markers solely to mark case; 127/156 languages with tense/aspect/mood markers used them solely to mark tense/aspect/mood). Thus in this way too English (and other Indo-European languages) are typologically unusual. However here they represent arguably the more complex case, such that systems developed for English or other Indo-European languages probably wouldn't need much if any adaptation to handle languages which express less information in each morpheme.

CHAPTER 3

Morphophonology

#23 The morphophonology of a language describes the way in which surface forms are related to underlying, abstract sequences of morphemes.

The previous chapter has alluded in several places to the fact that phonological processes apply to morphologically complex words, giving 'surface' forms which are not transparently related to the underlying sequence of morphemes which they represent. The collection of these rules in a language is its 'morphophonology'. Linguists discover the morphemes of a language by comparing the forms of many different words, collected either from corpora or by *elicitation* with speakers of the language. In the easiest case, linguists have access to or elicit *paradigms*, or the full set of inflected forms for a handful of representative roots alongside information about the grammatical contexts each form is appropriate for.[1] They then compare the different forms within and across paradigms to each other to establish which portions (or aspects, see #8–#9) of each form can be attributed to the root and which belong to other morphemes.

In many cases, morphemes (both roots and affixes) expressing the same information take slightly or significantly different forms in different words. When this happens, linguists determine whether the forms can be related to each other by regular (and 'natural') phonological rules.[2] This in turn requires positing an underlying form from which the surface forms are derived. This chapter briefly outlines three major types of morphophonological processes: those that involve only the forms of the morphemes (#24), those that involve the morphological identity of the morphemes (#25) and those where the surface form switches idiosyncratically to something completely different (#26). Finally, #27 discusses the relationship between orthography and phonology.

#24 The form of a morpheme (root or affix) can be sensitive to its phonological context.

Perhaps the most straightforward cases of morphemes changing their shape are the ones where it's simply the phonological context (the sounds of the surrounding morphemes) which triggers the change. A simple example of this comes from the English morphemes with the spelling

---

[1]In some languages, however, this is difficult to impossible. Gazdar and Mellish [1989, 59-60] calculate that Finnish verbs have about 12,000 forms and Hankamer [1989] that Turkish verbs have millions. In such cases, linguistic analysis proceeds by starting with the simpler forms rather than looking for complete paradigms.
[2]Not all approaches to phonology involve positing rules. Optimality Theory [Prince and Smolensky, 1993] is an example of a prominent constraint-based approach. Despite not using rules, it still relates underlying forms to surface forms.

-s (plural on nouns, third person singular present tense on verbs). This morpheme is pronounced as /s/, /z/, or /əz/ depending on the sound that precedes it. If the preceding sound is a voiceless consonant (like /t/, /p/ or /f/) the *-s* is pronounced /s/. If it's a voiced consonant (like /d/, /b/ or /v/) or a vowel, the *-s* is pronounced /z/. And if it's a sibilant (/s/, /z/, /ʃ/, /ʒ/, /tʃ/ or /dʒ/) it's pronounced /əz/.

(25) a. /s/: cats, caps, laughs

b. /z/: bids, cabs, believes

c. /əz/: buses, buzzes, caches, garages, birches, bridges

If we posit /z/ as the underlying form of these morphemes, these changes are all happening adjacent to the morpheme boundary. However, this is not always the case. An example of a long-distance change in the form of a morpheme comes from a process called 'vowel harmony' in Turkish. As shown in (26) (from Göksel and Kerslake 2005:23), the ablative case marker surfaces as *-dan* or *-den*, depending on the vowel in the root.[3]

(26) -dAn: ablative

hava-dan	'from the air'	ev-den	'from the house'
kız-dan	'from the girl'	biz-den	'from us'
yol-dan	'by the road'	göl-den	'from the lake'
şun-dan	'of this'	tür-den	'of the type'

[tur]

As noted above, Turkish can have long strings of suffixes. Many of the suffixes are subject to vowel harmony, giving rise to forms like those in (27):[4]

(27) a. üzüldünüz
üz-ül-dü-nüz
sadden-PASS-PST-2PL

'You became sad.' [tur] [Göksel and Kerslake, 2005, 22]

b. sevildiniz
sev-il-di-niz
like-PASS-PST-2PL

'You were liked.' [tur]

The examples so far have involved the form of the affix changing according to phonological properties of the root (or stem) it is attaching to. Roots can change as well. An example comes from Japanese verbs [Hinds, 1986, 420]:

---

[3]Here, the vowel's underlying form is posited as simply underspecified between *e* and *a*, written *A*.
[4]Example (27b) was provided by an anonymous reviewer.

(28)

stem	gloss	non-past	past
tabe-	'eat'	tabe-ru	tabe-ta
nom-	'drink'	nom-u	non-da
oyog-	'swim'	oyog-u	oyoi-da
erab-	'choose'	erab-u	eran-da
kak-	'write'	kak-u	kai-ta
nar-	'become'	nar-u	nat-ta

[jpn]

Here the form of the past tense (or completive aspect) varies between *-ta* and *-da* depending on the phonology of the root, but at the same time, the form of the root itself varies between non-past and past tense forms, for some verb classes.

Thus morphological analyzers and any NLP systems that involve features meant to recognize morphemes within words should be prepared to handle morphemes that vary in their form, including cases where the variation is not at the morpheme boundary.

#25 The form of a morpheme (root or affix) can be sensitive to its morphological context.

The form changes in #24 all relate to and are motivated by the phonological context. There are also alternations in morpheme form (cases of *allomorphy*) where the conditioning context is strictly morphological, i.e., depends on the identity rather than the form of the combining morphemes. The verbal inflection (or conjugation) classes of Latin and its descendants provide a clear example. (29) shows the present tense indicative paradigms for three verbs in French representing three regular verb inflection classes [Trager, 1955].[5] The key thing to note in this example is the different forms of the affixes for the different verb classes. The choice of form depends on the class of the verb, and the verb classes aren't defined in terms of the root's phonology; rather, class membership is an arbitrary lexical property of each verb.[6]

---

[5]Trager identifies a fourth class of *-oir* verbs.

[6]The data in (29) are presented in their standard orthographic forms. The patterns of homography (shared spellings) are different from the patterns of homophony (shared pronunciations); see #27.

(29)

	-er	-ir	-re
Infinitival form	manger	choisir	descendre
Gloss	'eat'	'choose'	'descend'
1sg	mang+e	chois+is	descend+s
2sg	mang+es	chois+is	descend+s
3sg	mang+e	chois+it	descend+
1pl	mang+eons	chois+issons	descend+ons
2pl	mang+ez	chois+issez	descend+ez
3pl	mang+ent	chois+issent	descend+ent

[fra]

Stems can also change based on morphological contexts in ways that are not phonologically predictable. French again provides an example with the verb *aller* 'to go'. Some inflected forms for this verb have the stem *all-*, as the infinitival form *aller* would suggest. However, the future and conditional forms all involve the stem *ir-* instead, as illustrated in (30):[7]

(30)　a.　Nous allons.

　　　　nous　all-ons

　　　　we　　go-1PL.PRES

　　　　'We go.' [fra]

　　　b.　Nous irons.

　　　　nous　ir-ons

　　　　we　　go-1PL.FUT

　　　　'We will go.' [fra]

#26 Suppletive forms replace a stem+affix combination with a wholly different word.

Above we have seen cases where stems and affixes take different forms in different inflected words. These changes can be related to the form or the morphological identity of the other morphemes in the word. In all of the cases noted above, however, it is still possible to identify substrings of the word as stem and affix respectively. Yet another twist on the realization of inflected words involves cases where the inflected form is unrelated to any other forms of the stem and affix and there is no way to divide the form up into its component morphemes. The English form *went* is a clear example of this phenomenon: This is the past tense of the verb *go*, but bears no resemblance to either the stem *go* or the past-tense morpheme *-ed*.

While suppletion of this type (where the whole form is different from the stem+affix) is likely to be fairly rare in terms of word types, there is reason to believe that such irregularities

---

[7]Suppletive forms are irregular, in that they cannot be generated by rule and must be memorized for each lexical item. Despite the *-er* ending, *aller* is therefore not a member of the first class in (29).

can only be maintained in high-frequency words [Bybee, 1985, Phillips, 2001]. Thus even while affecting only a small number of words, suppletion might have a high enough token frequency to affect system performance. Conversely, because only a small number of forms is typically involved, it is likely often inexpensive to add this linguistic knowledge directly to NLP systems.

#27 Alphabetic and syllabic writing systems tend to reflect some but not all phonological processes.

The preceding discussion has focused on the relationship between the pronunciation of fully inflected words and abstract underlying forms. Most of the examples have been presented in the standard orthography of the language in question and/or in a transliteration based on that orthography. The relationship between orthography and pronunciation is not straightforward, and varies from language to language. In some cases, orthography abstracts away from phonological processes. The example of English plural forms cited in #24 illustrates this nicely: The pronunciation of the regular plural affix takes three forms: /s/, /z/ and /əz/, while the spelling takes only two: *s* and *es*. Furthermore, the orthographic form *es* does not reliably indicate the pronunciation /əz/: compare *potatoes* and *foxes*.

In other cases, orthography can lag behind phonological processes, reflecting the pronunciation of an earlier stage of the language. Thus in the French paradigm for *manger* 'eat' presented in (29) above, the forms *mang+e*, *mang+es*, and *mang+ent* are all pronounced /mɑ̃ʒ/.[8] Where French orthography marks distinctions which aren't preserved in the spoken language, the standard orthographies for Arabic and Hebrew do not indicate most vowels, creating wide-spread homography between sets of inflected forms of the same root.

If morphophonology concerns the pronunciation of inflected forms and orthography only indirectly reflects pronunciation, one might hope that morphophonology is not relevant for NLP work that focuses on text only. Unfortunately, this is not the case. All of the kinds of processes described in this chapter are reflected in the orthography of at least some language, at least some of the time. Accordingly, NLP systems should be prepared for this kind of variation in linguistic form in addition to further noise introduced by the imperfect reflection of phonology in orthography.

---

[8]Though note that some French consonants which are otherwise 'silent' at the end of words do get pronounced when the following word starts with a vowel, and under certain syntactic and stylistic conditions, in the process called *liaison* [Klausenburger, 1984, Tseng, 2003].

CHAPTER 4

Morphosyntax

#28 The morphosyntax of a language describes how the morphemes in a word affect its combinatoric potential.

To recap so far: a *morpheme* is a minimal pairing of form and meaning in a language, and *morphology* is the study of how those pieces combine together to form words. Chapter 2 described several ways in which both the 'form' and 'meaning' part of the form-meaning pairing can differ from the simplest case. Chapter 3 explored morphophonology, or the ways in which the form of a morpheme can vary depending on its morphological and phonological context. This chapter is concerned with a specific subset of 'meanings' associated with morphemes, namely, those which reflect grammatical properties of the word and constrain its possible distribution within syntactic structures.

The term *morphosyntax* is ambiguous. On the one hand, it can be used to describe the totality of morphological and syntactic systems or facts within a language (or the study of those systems). This is the sense in which it was used in #1–#3 above. Here, it is used in a narrower sense to refer to those aspects of morphology which interface with syntax (as opposed to those which interface with phonology).

By providing an overview of various kinds of information which are expressed in inflectional morphology, the goal of this chapter is to convince the reader that morphological complexity is not there just to increase data sparsity. Rather, in languages with elaborate inflectional morphology especially, the differences in word form encode information which can be highly relevant to NLP tasks. Furthermore, given the existence of nearly perfectly isolating languages (see #20), anything that can be expressed morphologically in some language is likely to be expressed via periphrastic means (i.e., through a string of separate words) in some other language.[1]

#29–#37 briefly explain and illustrate a range of types of information that are marked morphologically in some languages. #38–#41 explore the phenomenon of *agreement* whereby the inflection of one word in the sentence depends on the morphosyntactic properties of another. Finally, #42 and #43 conclude the chapter with some reflections on cross-linguistic variation in morphosyntax.

---

[1]This is not necessarily always true, however: Languages vary in which aspects of meaning are 'grammaticalized' in the sense of being expressed through a particular function morpheme, either affix or independent word. This means that it is logically possible for something to be grammaticalized as an affix certain languages and not grammaticalized at all in the more isolating languages.

#29 Morphological features associated with verbs and adjectives (and sometimes nouns) can include information about tense, aspect and mood.

Tense, aspect and mood are three frequently grammaticalized properties of events which are commonly expressed via inflection on verbs. Comrie [1985] defines *tense* as "grammaticalized location in time" and *aspect* as "grammaticalization of expression of internal temporal consistency" (p. 9). Thus tense has to do with the location of the event being referred to with respect to time (utterance time or some other reference time, see Reichenbach 1947), whereas aspect relates to the way the event itself takes place over time. For example, the past tense in (31a) shows that the event being described took place in the past. The progressive aspect in that same example takes a viewpoint on the event as one with internal structure, whereas (31b) describes an event that is completed without reference to the internal structure.

(31)   a. He was walking to the store.

        b. He walked to the store.

Palmer [2001] defines *mood* as the inflectional realization of the category of modality. *Modality*, in turn, "is concerned with the status of the proposition that describes the event" (*Ibid.*, p. 1). Categories described as kinds of modality include *realis* and *irrealis* (whether or not the proposition is known by the speaker to be true; whether or not the speaker is asserting the proposition), as well as more specific categories such as *optative* (intention). Tense, aspect and mood are also closely related to each other. Many languages will have single morphemes which express both tense and aspect (e.g., a 'past perfective') or use a mood category, such as irrealis in the expression of future events.

Tense and aspect are very commonly marked via inflection. Dahl and Velupillai surveyed 222 languages for tense marking, and found that 110 had an inflectional future/non-future distinction, 134 had an inflectional past/non-past distinction, and only 53 had neither (2011a, 2011b). Looking in the same sample at the high level distinction between perfective aspect (marking completed events) and imperfective aspect (on-going, habitual or future events), they found 101 languages that had grammatical marking through inflection or through periphrasis of this aspectual distinction (2011c).

Tense and aspect are a particularly vexed area for crosslinguistic comparison [Poulson, 2011]. It is common to find partial overlap across languages in the range of meanings assigned to each form. An example from a pair of closely related languages comes from English and German, both of which have a present perfect form, but use them slightly differently. The German form is compatible with with past, present or future adverbs, whereas the English present perfect seems to take only present adverbs. In the examples in (32) from [Musan, 2001, 361], only (32b) uses the present perfect in the English translation.

(32) a. Hans   hat   gestern den   Brief   geschrieben.
          Hans.NOM have.3SG.PRES yesterday the.SG.ACC letter.SG.ACC write.PTCP

      'Hans wrote the letter yesterday.' [deu]

      b. Hans   hat   jetzt den   Brief   geschrieben.
          Hans.NOM have.3SG.PRES now the.SG.ACC letter.SG.ACC write.PTCP

      'Hans has finished writing the letter now.' [deu]

      c. Hans   hat   morgen den   Brief   geschrieben.
          Hans.NOM have.3SG.PRES tomorrow the.SG.ACC letter.SG.ACC write.PTCP

      'Hans will have finished writing the letter tomorrow.' [deu]

Even within one language, the relationship between morphological tense and the actual location of an event in time can be difficult. For example, English uses the present tense with past reference in the 'historical present' (33a), the present tense with future reference in examples like (33b) and past tense with non-past reference in sequence of tense examples like (33c):

(33) a. President Lincoln is heading to the theater to take in his last play.

      b. We are leaving tomorrow.

      c. She said she was a doctor.

Note also that differences in tense can signal differences unrelated or only indirectly related to time. Looking at scientific papers, de Waard [2010] found that verb form (tense and aspect) is highly correlated with whether a statement is part of the conceptual narrative of the paper or whether it is reporting on the actual experiment carried out.

While tense/aspect/mood are most commonly associated with verbal inflection, there are a handful of cases where it's the morphology on a noun expressing an argument of a verb that marks the tense of the clause. An example of this comes from Kayardild, a language of Australia. Bickel and Nichols [2011a] cite the data in (34) from Evans 1995, where the only difference is in the inflection on the noun. This difference must therefore somehow carry the tense information as well.

(34) a. Ngada   kurri-nangku   mala-y.
          1SG.NOM see-NEG.POTENTIAL sea-LOC.ACTUAL

      'I could not see the sea.' [gyd]

      b. Ngada   kurri-nangku   mala-wu.
          1SG.NOM see-NEG.POTENTIAL sea-PROPRIETIVE.FUT

      'I won't (be able to) see the sea.' [gyd]

To summarize, it is very common for languages to mark temporal information in verbal morphology. This information can provide an indirect indicator of the temporal relationship of the described event to the utterance time and the speaker's viewpoint on the event. The latter can be relevant to the relationship of described events to each other as in *Kim was walking to the store when it started raining*. In multilingual applications, and especially MT, it is important to note that the range of temporal meanings marked by even similar appearing categories need not be the same across languages.

#30 Morphological features associated with nouns can contribute information about person, number and gender.

Person, number and gender (or noun class) are three frequently grammaticalized properties commonly associated with nouns.[2] The grammatical property of *person* indicates the relation of the referent of a noun (or noun phrase) to the speaking event. Reference to the speaker or groups including the speaker is first person, reference to the addressee and not the speaker (but possibly also others) is second person, and reference to entities which are neither the speaker nor the addressee is third person. All languages have ways of referring to speakers, addressees and others, though not all languages have any morphological expression of these distinctions [Drellishak, 2009, Siewierska, 2004]. Some languages make further distinctions among first person non-singular forms. The most common of these is the *inclusive/exclusive* distinction, which provides a way of distinguishing first person plural reference which includes the addressee ('we' as in you and I, and possibly someone else) and that which does not ('we' as in me and someone else, but not you) [Cysouw, 2003].

The grammatical property of *number* is related to the cardinality of the set picked out by the referent. In English, a *singular* noun phrase refers to a single individual, while a *plural* noun phrase refers to a set with zero or more than one individuals (e.g., *We have no bananas.*). Some languages do not mark number at all. Others have more elaborate systems than English. Possible numbers include *dual* (two individuals), *trial* (three), *paucal* (a small number more than one), and *plural* (more than some specified minimum, depending on the system). In addition, some languages distinguish *greater and lesser* subcategories of *paucal* and/or *plural*. The meaning of *paucal* and *plural* will depend on which other categories the language contrasts with them [Corbett, 2000, Kibort and Corbett, 2008].

Wambaya (a language of Australia) has a three-way number distinction between singular, dual and plural. While the singular number can sometimes be used with plural and (less frequently) dual referents, noun phrases with overt dual marking refer unambiguously to sets containing two individuals [Nordlinger, 1998]. The example in (35) illustrates the category dual (glossed as 'DU') which is not only marked on the noun but also reflected in the agreement on the auxiliary verb (see #38):

---

[2]Though they can also be marked on other elements of the sentence, through agreement, see #38 below.

(35)   Jany-buli-ji wurlu-ng-a   nyurrunyurru.
       dog-DU-LOC 3.DU.A-1.O-NF chase

       'Two dogs chased me.' [wmb] [Nordlinger, 1998, 74]

Gender, or more generally noun class, is a third grammatical property associated with nouns in many languages. In languages with grammatical gender, all nouns are assigned to a particular noun class, and this class is reflected in morphological properties of other elements in the sentence that agree with nouns [Corbett, 1991]. For example, French has a two-class gender system, where all nouns are classified as *masculine* or *feminine*, and this property affects the form of determiners and adjectives co-occurring with the noun:

(36)   a. Voici   une   petite   voiture.
         Here.is INDEF.SG.F small.SG.F car.SG.F

         'Here is a small car.' [fra]

       b. Voici   un   petit   camion.
         Here.is INDEF.SG.M small.SG.M truck.SG.M

         'Here is a small truck.' [fra]

German has a three-class gender system, where the classes are masculine, feminine and neuter. Wambaya has a four-class system, with nouns referring to animates divided between masculine and feminine classes and nouns referring to inanimates divided between a 'vegetable' class and a neuter or other class [Nordlinger, 1998]. Bantu languages (a family of Africa including Swahili, Zulu, and many others) and Niger-Congo languages more generally, are notorious for having elaborate noun class systems [Katamba, 2003].[3] According to Katamba, the language from this group with the largest number of noun classes is Ganda, with 21 (though most of those are paired into singular and plural versions of what can be considered abstractly the same class).

In all cases, the gender assignment of a word is a lexical property of the word. For some words, properties of the real-world referent motivate the classes (e.g., French *femme* 'woman' is feminine, Wambaya *buranringma* 'wild orange' is vegetable) but other words are classified arbitrarily (e.g., French *lune* 'moon' is feminine while German *Mond* 'moon' is masculine; German *Mädchen* 'girl' is neuter). This contrasts with the notion of gender in English pronouns, which distinguish gender in the third person singular forms only (feminine *she*, masculine *he* and neuter *it*). In English, the choice of pronoun reflects properties of the real-world referent and does not depend on the lexical identity of any linguistic antecedent.

While person, number and gender are frequently grouped together as a class of linguistic properties, both by languages marking them with single morphemes and by linguists analyzing agreement, there are also differences among them. Where person and gender are typically inherent properties of nouns and pronouns, number is more typically added via inflection (on the noun itself

---

[3]For an example from Swahili, see #38 below.

or some agreeing element).[4] Person and number are similar in that they are relatively semantically stable across languages (where there are differences, it is relatively easy to describe them), where gender is widely variable.

The three properties are relevant to coreference resolution of pronouns (in languages where pronouns mark these distinctions), to the correct generation of pronouns (e.g., in MT, see Le Nagard and Koehn 2010), and also to agreement, which in turn is relevant to the generation of well-formed strings as well as the automatic detection of dependency structure in many languages.

#31 Morphological features associated with nouns can contribute information about case.

Where person, number and gender are related to the referent (and/or the lexical identity) of a noun phrase, the grammatical property of *case* concerns the relationship between the noun phrase and the sentence it appears in [Blake, 2001]. Not all languages have case, and those that do vary both in the number of cases that they distinguish and in the range of types of relationships marked with case.

The most minimal systems only contrast two different cases and associate these cases with different core argument positions. English is an extreme example of this, contrasting only nominative (*I, we, he, she, they*) and accusative (*me, us, him, her, them*) cases, only in pronouns, and in fact only in some pronouns (*you* and *it* don't vary with case). English uses the nominative forms for the subjects of finite verbs and accusative forms elsewhere.[5]

More complex case systems contrast more distinct cases, mark case on all noun phrases (not just pronouns) and use specific cases for noun phrases functioning as specific kinds of modifiers (rather than as arguments, see #53).[6] A language with a particularly exuberant case system is Finnish, with 15 cases [Karlsson, 1983], many of which indicate particular locations or directions of movement, as in (37),[7] where the ablative (ABL) and allative (ALL) cases on 'chair' and 'couch' indicate which is the source and which is the goal of the movement.

(37) a. Riitta   hyppäsi   tuolilta   sohvalle.
          Riita   hyppä-si   tuoli-lta   sohva-lle.
          Riita.NOM   jump-PST   chair-ABL   couch-ALL

      'Riitta jumped from the chair to the couch.' [fin]

---

[4]Though there are some nouns with inherent number, such as *scissors, goggles, pajamas, dregs, odds-and-ends, regalia*, and *condolences* which are inherently plural [Huddleston and Pullum, 2002, p. 340–345].

[5]The exceptions to this generalization involve cases of variation where both nominative and accusative are found depending on dialect and/or style [Huddleston and Pullum, 2002, 458–467]. Some authors refer to the possessive pronouns (e.g., *my, your, their*) and/or the possessive clitic *'s* as 'genitive case' in English. However, *'s* is probably best treated as a separate word [Sag et al., 2003, Ch. 6] and the possessive pronouns can just be treated as determiners.

[6]It is fairly common to find that one case is marked with a null or zero affix, in contrast to the remaining cases which are marked with specific additional morphemes.

[7](37a) is from Vainikka 1993. Thanks to Seppo Kittilä for providing (37b) and the segmentation of both examples.

b. Riitta   hyppäsi   tuolille   sohvalta
  Riitta   hyppä-si   tuoli-lle sohva-lta
  riitta.NOM jump-PST chair-ALL couch-ABL

'Riitta jumped to the chair from the couch.' [fin]

Case is a relatively common phenomenon in the world's languages. Iggesen [2011a] examined a sample of 261 languages and found that only 81 had no morphological case marking. The cases systems in the survey range from two-way contrasts through the 21-case system of Hungarian [Iggesen, 2011b].[8]

The functions of case will be elaborated in #80 below. For now it is important to note that the case of a noun phrase can be marked on the head noun itself and/or (via agreement, see #40) on the other elements of the noun phrase.

#32 Negation can be marked morphologically.

Dryer [2011c] surveyed 1,159 languages and found that every one of them has some way to mark sentential or standard negation as in (38), where (38b) is the negation of (38a).

(38)   a. Kim ate the whole pizza.

       b. Kim didn't eat the whole pizza.

In all languages in Dryer's sample, the expression of negation involved a morpheme of some type. This contrasts with, for example, the expression of yes-no questions, which doesn't have dedicated morphological expression in many languages. For present purposes, the most relevant observation in Dryer's study is that, in 396 of the languages, the morpheme in question is an affix that attaches to the verb. Dryer illustrates this with the following example from Kolyma Yukaghir, a language spoken in Siberia (example from Maslova 2003:492):

(39)   met numö-ge el-jaqa-te-je
      1SG house-LOC NEG-achieve-FUT-INTR.1SG

'I will not reach the house.' [yux]

More widely spoken languages which share this property include Japanese, Turkish, Farsi, and Tamil.

An additional 21 languages have both negation via independent words and negation with an affix. Though Dryer doesn't include English in this class, if we treat -*n't* as an affix, it should be:

(40)   a. Kim didn't eat the whole pizza.

       b. Kim did not eat the whole pizza.

---

[8]Hungarian and Finnish are both Finno-Ugric languages.

Another 120 languages use two morphemes together to mark negation, and in some of these, at least one of the morphemes is an affix (though Dryer does not break down this class).

Negation detection is important for many kinds of NLP applications, including sentiment analysis [e.g., Councill *et al.* 2010, Wiegand *et al.* 2010], symptom/diagnosis detection in medical records [e.g., Mitchell *et al.* 2004] and others. While simple sentential negation is not the only type of negation such applications must handle, it is a frequent one. Any system attempting to approach these tasks in a cross-linguistically applicable fashion will need to anticipate the possibility of negation being marked as affixes as well as separate words indicating negation.

#33 Evidentiality can be marked morphologically.

Evidentiality is a grammatical category which encodes the speakers' source of evidence for an assertion [de Haan, 2011b]. Cross-linguistically, evidential markers can be divided into *direct* and *indirect* evidentials, where direct evidentials signal that the speaker has direct sensory evidence for the truth of the asserted proposition and indirect evidentials indicate that the speaker is inferring the truth from some other facts or is reporting something that s/he heard from someone else. (41) provides an example of each type from Turkish (from Aksu-Koç and Slobin 1986, cited in de Haan 2011b):

(41)   a.   Ahmet geldi.
            Ahmet gel-di.
            Ahmet come-PST.DIR.EVD

            'Ahmet came.' (witnessed by the speaker) [tur]

       b.   Ahmet gelmiş.
            Ahmet gel-miş.
            Ahmet come-PST.INDIR.EVD

            'Ahmet came.' (unwitnessed by the speaker) [tur]

In de Haan's sample of 418 languages, 237 had grammaticalized evidentials of some type. Those that had direct evidentials (71 languages) also had indirect evidentials, though 166 languages only grammaticalize indirect evidentiality. de Haan [2011a] finds that among languages that mark evidentiality, the most common means of doing so is via a verbal affix or clitic.

The information encoded in evidentials could be useful for sentiment analysis and other applications that read in review-type data, as well as applications concerned with extracting event descriptions and timelines from free text (including both medical and intelligence applications). MT systems mapping between languages with and without evidentials would ideally learn how to map to appropriate periphrastic forms in the non-evidential language (e.g., *reportedly* for an indirect evidential) and vice versa. Similarly, between two languages with evidentials, it would be important to get the mapping right.

#34 Definiteness can be marked morphologically.

The grammatical category of *definiteness* pertains to the status of referents with respect to the common ground of the interlocutors. An *indefinite* noun phrase introduces a referent that the speaker does not expect the addressee to already know of or be able to uniquely identify on first mention. A *definite* noun phrase, by contrast, picks out a referent that has already been introduced into the discourse or which the speaker expects the listener can uniquely identify on the basis of the description in the definite noun phrase [Gundel *et al.*, 1993].[9]

In English, definiteness is marked via the determiner within a noun phrase. Indefiniteness can be marked with *a* or *some* or (for plurals) no determiner. Definiteness can be expressed by *the*, demonstratives (*that, this*) or possessive determiners (*their, Kim's*). In his (2011a, 2011b) surveys of languages for definite and indefinite articles, Dryer found 92 languages (of 620 surveyed) that have nominal affixes marking definites and 24 languages (of 534 surveyed) with nominal affixes marking indefinites. Dryer illustrates these affixal marking strategies with the examples in (42a) and (42b) (from Gary and Gamal-Eldin 1982:59 and van Enk and de Vries 1997:75 respectively). (42a) is from Egyptian Arabic and (42b) is from Korowai, a Trans-New Guinea language spoken in Indonesia.

(42) a. ʔiṭ-ṭajjaar-a   gaaja
          DEF-plane-F.SG come

          'The plane is coming.' [arz]

      b. uma-té-do   abül-fekha khomilo-bo
          tell-3PL.REAL-DS man-INDEF die.3SG.REAL-PERF

          'They told that a certain man had died.' [khe]

Other languages that use this morphological strategy for definites include Hebrew, many varieties of Arabic, Norwegian, Danish, and Swedish.

Definiteness is relevant to coreference resolution, both in establishing (and delimiting) chains of coreferent NPs in discourse [see Mitkov 1998, Ng and Cardie 2002] and in grounding the reference of such chains to real-world entities.

#35 Honorifics can be marked morphologically.

Another grammatical category that is present in some but not all languages is honorifics. Honorifics mark social status, especially relative to the speaker, of either the addressee or a referent in the sentence, as well as lending formality to the social situation. (For an overview of the functions of honorifics and how they have been analyzed, see Agha 1994.) Honorifics can include

---

[9]There can be many ways in which a referent can become uniquely identifiable, including by virtue of being unique (*the sun*), by virtue of being introduced by a long definite description (*the pen on the table next to the magazine*) and by relying on accommodation by the addressee, who, on hearing *the dog ate my homework*, can assume that the speaker has a dog as a pet [see Lewis 1979].

terms of address, choice of pronoun for second-person referents, alternative lexical forms of nouns and verbs, as well as both nominal and verbal inflection.

Japanese has a particularly elaborate system of honorifics, as exemplified in (43), adapted from Yamaji 2000:191.

(43)　a.　先生　　が　太郎　を　助けた。
　　　　　Sensei　ga　Taroo wo　tasuke-ta
　　　　　Teacher NOM Taro　ACC help-PST

　　　　　'The teacher assisted Taro.' [jpn]

　　　b.　先生　　が　太郎　を　お助け　　に　なった。
　　　　　Sensei　ga　Taroo wo　o-tasuke　ni　nat-ta
　　　　　Teacher NOM Taro　ACC HON-help DAT become-PST

　　　　　'The teacher assisted Taro.' [jpn]

　　　c.　先生　　が　太郎　を　助けました。
　　　　　Sensei　ga　Taroo wo　tasuke-mashi-ta
　　　　　Teacher NOM Taro　ACC help-HON=PST

　　　　　'The teacher assisted Taro.' [jpn]

　　　　　先生　　が　太郎　を　お助け　　に　なりました。
　　　　　Sensei　ga　Taroo wo　o-tasuke　ni　nari-mashi-ta
　　　　　Teacher NOM Taro　ACC HON-help DAT become-HON-PST

　　　　　'The teacher assisted Taro.' [jpn]

The morpheme -mashi- in (43b,d) expresses politeness towards the addressee, while the o-… ni nat-ta frame is a referent honorific, related to the social status of the subject (sensei).[10]

Honorifics may seem far removed from core dependencies (who did what to whom), but in fact they can be relevant for NLP systems. On the one hand, they can provide useful constraints on coreference resolution, especially of pronominal or dropped arguments (see #96). On the other hand, they can provide information regarding the intended addressee of an utterance as well as about the genre/style of a text. They can also be of critical importance in applications requiring natural language generation, as they play a big role in shaping the perception of the machine as a polite, appropriate interlocutor.

#36 Possessives can be marked morphologically.

A *possessive* construction expresses a relationship between entities denoted by noun phrases. In English, possessives are expressed by possessive pronouns (*my, your, his/her/its, our, their*), by the possessive clitic *'s* (see #19), and by the preposition *of* as in *the end of the road*. Despite the

---

[10]Though, as Yamaji argues, in actual usage, Japanese speakers' choice to use referent honorifics is conditioned on their relationship to and attitude towards the addressee, as well as their relationship to the referent.

name, the relationship denoted by such constructions is not always one of ownership, but cover a much broader range. Langacker [1995, 56] identifies a wide range of relationships expressed by English possessives including relatives (*your aunt*), part-whole (*my knee*), physical qualities (*his height*) and associated entities (*our waiter*), among others.[11]

Cross-linguistically, the possessive construction can be indicated by morphology on the possessed noun, morphology on the possessor noun, both, simple juxtaposition without further marking, or by a separate word [Nichols and Bickel, 2011]. In English, the marking is associated with the possessor noun phrase, which can be a possessive pronoun (*my, your,* etc.) or a noun phrase marked with the clitic *'s* (see #19). The Chechen (Nakh-Daghestanian, Russia) examples in (44) illustrate the case where the marking is on the possessed noun:

(44)   a.   loem-an k'orni
            lion-GEN baby.animal

            'lion cub', 'lion's cub' (lit. 'of-lion cub') [che]

       b.   mashien-an maax
            car-gen   price

            'the price of a car' (lit. 'of-car price') [che] [Nichols and Bickel, 2011]

In addition, the marking of possession can sometimes agree with (or indicate) person/number/gender information about one of the nouns. In English, the possessive pronouns indicate the person, number and gender of the possessor. In French, the possessive pronouns indicate the person and number of the possessor, but agree with the gender of the possessed noun:

(45)   a.   ma   voiture
            POSS.1SG.F car.F

            'my car' [fra]

       b.   mon   camion
            POSS.1SG.M car.M

            'my truck' [fra]

       c.   sa   voiture
            POSS.3SG.F car.F

            'his/her car' [fra]

       d.   son   camion
            POSS.3SG.M truck.M

            'his/her truck' [fra]

---

[11]Langacker's study looked primarily at English. It does not necessarily follow that possessive constructions in other languages have this same range of functions.

#37 Yet more grammatical notions can be marked morphologically.

The preceding discussion has highlighted a range of information which is commonly marked by morphological means in the world's languages and which can be highly relevant in various NLP applications. This discussion has not, however, exhausted the range of information which can be encoded via affixes. The following list gives a sense of other kinds of information marked morphologically, while still not being exhaustive:[12]

- Some morphemes mark lexical processes or alternations which add arguments to a verb (see #54), including *causatives* (#87) and *benefactives* (#82).

- Conversely, some morphemes mark lexical processes or alternations which reduce the number of arguments overtly expressed (e.g., *passives*, #84) or the number of real world participants involved (*reflexives, reciprocals*, #82).

- Some languages require specific morphology to construct *imperative* (command) or *interrogative* (question) clauses [Dryer, 2011e, van der Auwera *et al.*, 2011].

- Part of speech changing processes often have associated affixes. An important subtype of these is *nominalization*, a process by which event-denoting verbal expressions are turned into nominal expressions which can then participate in sentences in the way that noun phrases do [Koptjevskaja-Tamm, 2012].

In general, given the wide range of information that can be marked morphologically, when designing NLP systems which are meant to be language-independent, it is a good idea to step back and consider what kind of linguistic information is being captured and where in the string the system is looking for it. Features designed with a relatively isolating language like English in mind may not work as well for more highly inflecting languages.

#38 When an inflectional category is marked on multiple elements of sentence or phrase, it is usually considered to belong to one element and to express agreement on the others.

The preceding sections have focused on the inflection of individual words within sentences, but the information marked by inflectional morphology is closely related to the combinatoric potential of the inflected word forms. Consider the following Swahili example, adapted from Reynolds and Eastman 1989:64.

(46) Mi-ti   mi-kubwa hi-i   y-a   mwitu i-li-anguka jana.
      c4-trees c4-big   these-c4 of.c4-POSS forest c4-PST-fall yesterday.

   'These big trees of the forest fell yesterday.' [swh]

---

[12]Some of these types of information are considered to be in the realm of derivational, rather than inflectional, morphology (see #12).

The morphemes glossed 'c4' all are reflecting the fact that *miti* the word for 'trees' (plural) belongs to the noun class 4 (see #30). This is registered in the prefix of the noun itself, as well as in prefixes on the adjective modifying the noun (*mikubwa*, 'big'), the possessive word *ya*, the demonstrative *hii* 'these' and the verb. This phenomenon, whereby morphological properties of one word are reflected in the form of others, is called *agreement* [Corbett, 2006, Moravcsik, 1978].

The following discussion will elaborate more examples of agreement. In all cases, the agreement is between a head and a dependent. From the point of view of analysis (parsing), the existence of agreement means that information expressed by morphology isn't necessarily interpreted 'locally'. On the other hand, because agreement is closely tied to dependency structure, it can be beneficial for dependency parsing. From the point of view of generation, conversely, finding the correct form of words in morphologically complex languages can be aided by information about dependency structures [see Toutanova *et al.* 2008].

#39 Verbs commonly agree in person/number/gender with one or more arguments.

One common type of agreement is for verbs to reflect the person, number and/or gender of one or more of their arguments. Even English does this, to a tiny degree: The present tense form of English verbs depends on the person and number of the subject, taking the *-s* suffix if the subject is third person and singular and no suffix otherwise:[13]

(47)   a. He/she/it jumps.

     b. I/we/you/they jump.

In many other languages, systems of verb-argument agreement are more elaborate than what is found in English, distinguishing more combinations of person, number and gender and applying in all tenses.

In general, agreement of this type is wide-spread. Siewierska [2011c] surveyed the presence of agreement in person information across 378 languages, looking at both agreement with the agent (actor) and agreement with the patient (undergoer) arguments of transitive verbs, including both affixes and clitics as markers of agreement.[14] She found that only 82 languages did not mark agreement in person at all, and 193 marked agreement with both agent and patient.

Note that the English verb endings (*-s* and *-Ø*) also indicate tense information. It is common among Indo-European and Semitic languages for single morphemes to reflect both the tense/aspect/mood of the verb and agreement with an argument, though this pattern is less common in other language families [Bickel and Nichols, 2011a].

---

[13]The only exceptions to this pattern are the modals (which don't agree at all) and the verb *be*, which has three distinct forms in the present tense: *am* for first person singular subjects, *is* for third person singular subjects and *are* for all others. *Be* is also exceptional in being the only English verb to show agreement with the subject in the past tense, using *was* for first and third person singular and *were* for all other person-number combinations.

[14]The notions of 'subject' and 'object' are syntactic rather than semantic and furthermore not established as linguistic universals (see #70). For typological work it can be more straightforward to identify arguments based on (rough) semantic roles.

Finally, while both linguists and others often refer to forms like *jumps* as the 'third person singular form of the verb', this terminology is inaccurate and doesn't scale: It's inaccurate because it's not the verb that is third person and singular but rather its subject. It doesn't scale because there are languages in which verbs can agree with more than one argument at the same time.

#40 Determiners and adjectives commonly agree with nouns in number, gender and case.

Where verbs often agree with their (nominal) dependents, noun phrases the typical agreement pattern goes the other way, with the dependents (determiners, adjectives) agreeing with the head noun. Again, even English does this to a small degree: the demonstrative determiners agree in number with the nouns they modify:

(48)   a.   this/that book

   b.   these/those books

Similarly, in the Swahili example (46) above, three dependents of the noun *miti* 'trees' are inflected to agree with the head noun's noun class: the demonstrative *hi-i* 'these', the adjective *mikubwa* 'big', and the possessive marker *ya* 'of'.

Swahili doesn't have a case system, but German provides examples of determiner-noun and adjective-noun agreement in number, gender and case, as illustrated in (49):

(49)   Der   alte   Mann   gab   dem   kleinen
       The.M.SG.NOM old.M.SG.NOM man.M.SG.NOM gave.PST the.M.SG.DAT little.M.SG.DAT
       Affen   eine   grosse   Banane.
       monkey.M.SG.DAT a.SG.F.ACC big.SG.F.ACC banana.SG.F.ACC
       'The old man gave the little monkey a big banana.' [deu]

As indicated in the glosses here, each of the determiners expresses a particular combination of number, gender and case and likewise for each inflected form of the adjectives. The nouns have inherent gender and are inflected for number and case. Switching the determiners *der* and *dem*, for example, would lead to an ill-formed utterance. It would be unusual to find nominal dependents agreeing in person with a head noun, because the only nouns that are not third person are pronouns, and pronouns typically do not take determiners, adjectives or other dependents.

In most languages, noun phrases generally form contiguous substrings of a sentence, and so agreement properties are probably less important for recovering dependency relations between nouns and their associated determiners and adjectives.[15] There are languages, however, which allow discontinuous noun phrases, where modifiers frequently appear separated from the head noun by other clausal material (see #95).[16]

---

[15]Though note that agreement can still be useful for determining the boundaries of particular noun phrases.
[16]Even in English and other familiar languages like German relative clauses at least can be separated from their head nouns:

In these languages, agreement plays a crucial role in indicating the intended interpretation of a sentence. (50), from Nordlinger 1998:223, provides an example from Wambaya.

(50)   Ngaragana-nguja ngiy-a   gujinganjanga-ni jiyawu ngabulu.
       grog-PROP.IV.ACC 3.SG.NM.A-PST mother.II.ERG   give   milk.IV.ACC

       '(His) mother gave (him) milk with grog in it.' [wmb]

Here the affix *-nguja* on *ngaragana* 'grog' indicates that the word is functioning as a modifier meaning 'having grog' and that it modifies a noun that is class IV and accusative case. Here, that noun is *ngabulu* 'milk', found at the other end of the sentence.

#41 Agreement can be with a feature that is not overtly marked on the controller.

Swahili (like other Bantu languages) makes a good starting point for illustrating agreement because the markers involved appear on both the source (or 'controller', in Corbett's terminology) of the agreement and the targets, and furthermore, in many cases, the affixes even take the same form (see (46) above). However, it is very common to find cases of agreement where the marking is only overt on the target (i.e., the element that is agreeing with properties of some other word). For example, French determiners reflect the gender and number of the nouns they combine with. The gender is typically not marked on nouns via any affixes. The number is marked in the orthography, but not usually pronounced (see #27). This is illustrated in (51), where the determiners in (51a) and (51c) give the only overt indication of the gender of the nouns, and the determiners in all cases give the only phonologically available indication of the number.

(51)   a. Je vois   la   voiture.
          1SG see.1SG the.F.SG car.SG

          'I see the car.' [fra]

       b. Je vois   les   voiture-s.
          1SG see.1SG the.PL car-PL

          'I see the cars.' [fra]

       c. Je vois   le   camion.
          1SG see.1SG the.M.SG truck.SG

          'I see the truck.' [fra]

       d. Je vois   les   camion-s.
          1SG see.1SG the.PL truck-PL

          'I see the trucks.' [fra]

(i) A student walked in [who I had never met before].

Because the relevant features on the controller of agreement (here the nouns) aren't necessarily overtly marked in the morphology, if systems such as dependency parsers are going to take advantage of agreement, they require morphological analyzers which make this information explicit. This, in turn, requires that the morphological analyzers have access to lexical resources in which to look up these properties. Fortunately, in such languages, the agreement properties themselves make it reasonably easy to acquire such lexical resources automatically [Nicholson *et al.*, 2006].

Going even further, there are times when the agreement markers on one element (especially a verb) are the only information available about a particular argument, because the argument in question has been 'dropped' (see #96). (52), adapted from Bresnan and Mchombo 1987:747, provides an example from Chicheŵa, another Bantu language (spoken in Malawi and neighboring countries):

(52)   a. Fîsi   anagúlá chipéwá ku San Francíscó dzulo.
           hyena bought hat.c7   in San Francisco yesterday

           'The hyena bought a hat in San Francisco yesterday.' [nya]

       b. Madzŭlo anapítá ku San Jose kuméné **á-ná-ká-chí-gulítsá** kw'á m̑lóndá wá á
           evening he-went to San Jose where   CI-PST-**go**-C7-**sell** to   guard   of HON
           mêya.
           mayor

           'In the evening he went to San Jose, where he went to sell it to the mayor's guard.'
           [nya]

The arguments of the boldfaced verb in this short discourse are not expressed by any independent noun phrases. The only information provided about them is in the agreement markers (alternatively: pronominal affixes) on the verb. The noun class information helps to narrow down the possible antecedents. Examples like this highlight the importance of morphological analysis to coreference resolution.

#42 Languages vary in which kinds of information they mark morphologically.

This section and the next conclude this discussion of morphology by considering cross-linguistic variation. The preceding discussion has attempted to provide a sense of the range of kinds of information which can be marked via morphological means cross-linguistically. Typological studies cited provide evidence for the prevalence of particular kinds of inflectional morphology, but in every case also include non-trivial numbers of languages which do not mark the information in question via affixes.

Given the existence of isolating languages (see #20), there can be no information which is universally expressed via affixes. Some types of information, e.g., sentential negation, have grammaticalized or dedicated means of expression in all languages; those that don't use morphology use independent words. Other kinds of information, such as evidentials and honorifics, are only grammaticalized in some languages, and thus we find three broad types of languages in these categories: those that express evidentials/honorifics morphologically, those that use (only) separate words, and those that don't grammaticalize these notions, but can still express the same ideas through longer, non-standardized paraphrasing.

Note that information not grammaticalized in some languages (e.g., evidentials, honorifics, or noun class, none of which are grammaticalized in English) can be not only grammaticalized but in fact required in other languages. For example, utterances not bearing honorifics in Japanese are not neutral, but specifically marked as belonging to a certain level of formality. Thus in translating into a language it is important to know which kinds of information are obligatorily marked (via morphology or other means).

The World Atlas of Language Structures Online [Dryer and Haspelmath, 2011], cited extensively throughout this chapter, includes a database recording all of the individual classifications of languages underlying each of the surveys. Though not every language is included in every survey, this database can provide a first-pass description of the kinds of information a given language expresses morphologically.

#43 Languages vary in how many distinctions they draw within each morphologically marked category.

Even if two languages mark the same category with inflectional morphology, they can still vary, and vary widely, in terms of the number of distinctions they make within that category. For example, a minimal case system contrasts two cases. As was mentioned in #31 above, Hungarian has 21 different cases. Similarly, a minimal tense system contrasts two tenses, typically past and non-past or future and non-future. Dahl and Velupillai [2011b] surveyed 222 languages for past tense marking. In that sample, the language with the richest system of distinctions within the past tense was Yagua [Payne and Payne, 1990], with the five-way contrast outlined in (53).

(53)

Name of tense	Use
Proximate 1	'a few hours previous to the time of utterance'
Proximate 2	'one day previous to the time of utterance'
Past 1	'roughly one week ago to one month ago'
Past 2	'roughly one to two months ago up to one or two years ago'
Past 3	'distant or legendary past'

Similarly, a minimal number system contrasts two values, which can be singular and plural or plural and 'general number', i.e., a number value which is not specified as specifically singular or plural [see Corbett 2000]. The most elaborate number systems identified by Kibort and Corbett [2008] have five-way contrasts, marking singular, dual, trial, paucal and plural or singular, dual, paucal, greater paucal and plural. These systems are attested in Lihir, Sursurunga, and Tangga, all Oceanic languages of Papua New Guinea.[17]

The number of contrasts in a system potentially affects the semantic value of each term in the system. Accordingly, cross-linguistic comparison and translation needs to be done with care, and developers of NLP systems intended to function cross-linguistically should anticipate the morphological properties can take either more or fewer possible values in languages other than the development languages (when they are present at all). This section has focused on examples from resource-poor languages which are not widely spoken nor widely known, but these issues arise even between more familiar language pairs: English contrasts past, present and future in its tense system; Japanese has a two-way contrast between past and non-past.[18]

---

[17]The distinction between the two systems is whether there is a strict trial form which can only be used when the set of entities being referred to numbers three.

[18]Though this system is sometimes analyzed instead as aspect rather than tense [Soga, 1983].

CHAPTER 5

Syntax: Introduction

#44 Syntax places constraints on possible sentences.

This chapter provides an introduction to a series of chapters on syntax. Just as the morphology of a language provides a set of rules for constructing possible words out of smaller pieces, and determining the form and meaning of the resulting combinations, the syntax of a language can be viewed as a system of rules for constructing possible (grammatical, acceptable) sentences out of words, and determining their form (word sequence) and meaning. An important difference between morphology and syntax is that for most languages, a given set of lexical items (roots) can give rise to only finitely many word forms,[1] though of course new roots can always be coined. Most linguists hold that syntactic systems describe non-finite sets of strings using finitely many rules [e.g., Epstein and Hornstein 2005, Postal 1964].[2] This claim can be illustrated with sentences like *Some sentences go on and on and on.* [Sag *et al.*, 2003, 22], which can be made arbitrarily longer by adding *and on*.

Much work in theoretical syntax foregrounds the issue of grammaticality, concerning itself with distinguishing grammatical sentences from strings of words that do not constitute grammatical sentences. Theoretical syntacticians are interested in determining what kinds of formal mechanisms are required in order to be able to describe all existing natural languages in this way. In general, these questions are not directly relevant to NLP systems. Systems that are given text to process are typically not concerned with determining which of the strings in that text are grammatical. Furthermore, most NLP systems need to be robust to input which is ill-formed in various ways, because of typos, non-native speaker input, false starts and other properties of spoken language, and noise introduced by earlier stages of processing (e.g., speech recognition or sentence tokenization). The obvious exceptions are systems which need to generate text (where well-formed output is preferred) and systems specifically involved in grammar checking, which need to identify (and ideally diagnose) errors.

---

[1]The exception would be languages with particularly productive derivational morphology, with rules that can apply recursively to their own output.
[2]Not all linguists subscribe to this claim; see for example Pullum and Scholz 2010.

#45 Syntax provides scaffolding for semantic composition.

Other work on syntax (including both theoretical work and computational work on precision grammars[3]) is more focused on its role in determining the meaning of sentences. Here the interesting questions are in the design of the meaning representations and in the exploration of the syntactic devices (e.g., rule types) required to be able to compositionally arrive at those representations based on the words in the sentence and the way they are put together. This wording deliberately echoes 'Frege's principle', or the Principle of Compositionality, which can be stated as "The meaning of a complex expression is determined by its structure and the meaning of its constituents" [Szabó, 2008]. At one level, it seems that this must be true of language: all speakers are capable of producing and understanding sentences they have not previously encountered, and so there must be some way of arriving at meanings from unfamiliar strings and strings for new meanings. Nonetheless, it is challenged by such things as local non-compositionality (idiomatic expressions) and more importantly context-dependence of various types. Furthermore, there is strong evidence that listeners leverage a great deal information beyond the linguistic string in order to determine the communicative intent of their interlocutors [Clark, 1996]. In other words, the 'conduit metaphor', which holds that the speaker packs a message into a natural language sentence from which the listener unpacks it upon receipt, is not a good model for human communication; the strings uttered are just one type of cue to communicative intent, processed along with everything else available [Reddy, 1993].

Nonetheless, computational syntacticians have found it useful to assume a level of invariant semantic information associated with any given string. This information is never complete, but rather represents that which is common across all possible felicitous uses of the string and thus can be associated with the string itself. Prominent within this information is the familiar 'who did what to whom' of dependency structures (see #3), along with information about modifiers of both events and individuals, quantifiers, and semantic features such as number and tense. While much of this information can be associated with individual words within a sentence, the way that information is combined into semantic structures is highly dependent on syntax. Thus even though the same words are used in the same senses in (54a) and (54b), the meanings of the sentences are not the same:

(54)   a. The brown dog on the mat saw the striped cat through the window.

         b. The brown cat saw the striped dog through the window on the mat.

#46 Constraints ruling out some strings as ungrammatical usually also constrain the range of possible semantic interpretations of other strings.

While these two views of syntax may appear to be opposed to each other, they can also be complementary. Even work that is primarily concerned with grammaticality appeals to se-

---

[3]'Precision grammars' are computational grammars which are hand-crafted to reflect linguistic generalizations. For more on precision grammars, see #99.

mantic intuitions and sometimes looks to semantic constraints to explain the infelicity of certain kinds of sentences. Conversely, and from a computational point of view, modeling grammaticality can be important for parsing: constraints that rule out ungrammatical strings typically also rule out unwarranted analyses of grammatical strings. In parsing systems that include semantic representations (including systems which read so-called semantic dependencies off of syntactic phrase structure trees), each syntactic analysis is typically associated with a semantic representation. This means that an underconstrained grammar, which allows ungrammatical sentences, will likely also license unwarranted interpretations of grammatical sentences. Additionally, a smaller range of analyses for any given input entails a simpler parse selection problem, and better 1-best results, provided that the underlying grammar is not overconstrained to the point where the correct analysis is not available.

Both views of syntax, whether concerned with describing sets of possible sentences or with describing the ways in which words and their meanings can be combined to create sentences with associated meanings, share a common set of fundamental analytical concepts. These are introduced and illustrated in the following chapters, again with an eye towards cross-linguistic variation and towards relevance to NLP. Chapter 6 looks at parts of speech, or the classification of words based on their distribution and/or function. Chapter 7 takes up the notions of head, argument and adjunct, which are general names for roles that words can play in larger structures. Chapter 8 looks at the different kinds of semantic and syntactic arguments and how languages relate them to each other and Chapter 9 looks at various ways in which languages allow mismatches between syntactic and semantic arguments.

CHAPTER 6

Parts of speech

#47 Parts of speech can be defined distributionally (in terms of morphology and syntax).

Distributionally-defined part of speech categories group words together based on the morphological and syntactic contexts in which they appear [Schachter and Shopen, 2007]. Morphological distributional similarity involves being able to combine with the same set of affixes. Thus morphological evidence suggests that *walk*, *slice*, *donate* and *believe* all belong to the same part of speech in English, as they can all combine with the affixes *-s*, marking present tense and agreement with a third-person singular subject and *-ed* marking past tense (or the past participle). As noted in #24–#26, however, there is a great deal of lexical idiosyncrasy in the form of morphemes, so linguists typically look instead to the meaning of affixes that can attach to a given form. This allows us to include *sleep*, *eat* and *give*, among others in the category of verb, even though they don't take the *-ed* ending but instead mark past tense irregularly.[1]

Syntactic distributional similarity can be explored with *substitution tests*. At the most fine-grained level, words which can be substituted for each other while maintaining the grammaticality and overall structure of a sentence, belong to the same part of speech class:

(55) Kim saw the { elephant, movie, mountain, error } before we did.

Such tests can be too strict, however. We would like to say that *arrive* and *see* are both verbs, but *arrive* is intransitive and cannot be substituted for *see* in (55). Likewise, *elephant* and *Sandy* are both nouns, but *Sandy* is a proper noun and thus doesn't have the same distribution:

(56) a. *Kim arrived the { elephant, movie, mountain, error } before we did.

b. *Kim saw the Sandy before we did.

What these examples point out is the hierarchical nature of part of speech systems. Though the most commonly used part of speech tagsets are presented as flat sets of tags, in fact categories defined by the tags can usually be grouped together into broader categories, and conversely divided more finely into more specific categories.

---

[1]There is also the issue of homophones. That is, not all tokens of the same string type are necessarily instances of the same word type. English is particularly rife with part of speech straddling lexical ambiguity, with many stems functioning as both nouns and verbs and overlap in the inflectional forms as well, with the plural affix on nouns colliding with the third-person singular present tense affix on verbs.

The tagset for the Penn Treebank (considering only leaf nodes, not the tags on phrases) consists of 36 lexical tags and 12 additional tags for punctuation [Marcus *et al.*, 1993, 317].[2] It groups together all verbs regardless of transitivity, but distinguishes common nouns from proper nouns. At the same time, it also distinguishes nouns and verbs based on inflectional categories. NN (singular or mass common nouns) is a different tag from NNS (plural common nouns); VB (verb in the base form) is different from (VBD past tense verb), etc. All of this information (major part of speech, transitivity and valence more generally, and inflectional categories) can be useful for further processing and constrains the combinatoric potential of words. More flexible representations use attribute-value pairs to represent each piece of information separately, rather than packing it in to a single part of speech tag [see Bilmes and Kirchhoff 2003].

#48 Parts of speech can also be defined functionally (but not metaphysically).

Traditional school grammar defines parts of speech semantically (or 'metaphysically', to borrow Pullum's [2012] term[3]), with nouns referring to people, places or things, verbs to actions, and so on. As Pullum and many others point out, going back to at least Fries 1952, these metaphysical definitions are unsuitable because they are unoperationalizable in the general case. The typical solution is to rely on distributional factors, which can be clearly defined and operationalized as tests, as described in #47 above.

Another approach which is more semantic, yet not metaphysical, is to look at the semantic function of words in a sentence. Hengeveld [1992] lays out functional definitions of the four major parts of speech. He first defines verbs as those which in their primary use can only be used predicatively and nouns as those which in their primary use can be arguments.[4] He then defines adjectives and adverbs as those which, in their primary use, can modify nouns and verbs, respectively.

These functional definitions can be used together with distributional ones to create a basis for cross-linguistic comparison, which is of particular interest to typologists. Distributional characteristics are necessarily language-specific; the functional definitions are cross-linguistically applicable. Another approach to establishing comparable part of speech categories cross-linguistically involves lexical prototypes. Wierzbicka [2000] proposes labeling major part of speech categories based on words that are believed to occur in all languages. For example, the major part of speech class (established on language-internal distributional grounds) containing the translational equivalents of *say*, *see* and *hear* should be labeled 'verb'.

---

[2]This tagset was deliberately created to be less fine-grained than the Brown tagset [Francis and Kučera, 1982] on which it was based.

[3]Pullum's blog posts, both for the *Chronicle of Higher Education* (http://chronicle.com/blogs/linguafranca) and Language Log (http://languagelog.org) are generally delightfully witty and an interesting source of insight into the nature of language.

[4]This must exclude verbal projections which are arguments of other verbs, but it is not immediately clear how.

#49 There is no one universal set of parts of speech, even among the major categories.

Linguists distinguish between open and closed part of speech classes [Schachter and Shopen, 2007], where open classes readily accept new words and are generally larger classes. While the open classes can be compared cross-linguistically, and at least the verb and noun classes may be found in all languages (though even this is controversial, see Schachter and Shopen 2007), the set of closed classes is much more variable across languages.[5] The open classes generally include nouns, verbs, adjectives and adverbs. Some languages don't distinguish adjectives as a separate class, and languages differ in the distinctions they draw within these major classes. The closed classes include elements like pronouns, determiners, adpositions (prepositions or postpositions), interjections, numerals, numeral classifiers and 'particles'. 'Particle' is used in scare quotes here, as it appears to be used in the linguistics literature to label elements which do not belong to other part of speech classes in the language and whose part of speech is unclear.[6]

The claim that there is no universal set of part of speech classes can be more precisely formulated as follows: There is no set of part of speech classes (or tags) which can capture the relevant distinctions in all languages and for which each component class is attested in all languages. Thus the class of adjectives is clearly a separate class in many languages, but just as clearly not present in many others [Dixon 1977, but see Dixon 2004]. The same argument can be made about many other part of speech classes, especially closed classes like determiners. On the other hand, a relaxed version of the claim may be sustainable: That is, it may be possible to define a relatively small set of part of speech categories such that it is possible to define a mapping from the language-specific part of speech types for any language to that small set and the range of distinctions drawn by this universal inventory is sufficient for at least some practical purposes. The first part of this relaxed claim is trivially true if a) the universal inventory includes an 'other' or 'residue' class and b) we don't insist that every class in the inventory is instantiated in every language. The second part remains an empirical question.

This pragmatic approach is explored in Petrov *et al.* 2012, who define a set of 12 universal part of speech categories, and then map the annotations of 25 treebanks representing 22 languages to those categories. The categories are NOUN, VERB,verb ADJ (adjectives), ADV (adverbs), PRON (pronouns), DET (determiners and articles), ADP (prepositions and postpositions), CONJ (conjunctions), PRT (particles), . (punctuation), and X (everything else). These categories aren't given specific definitions; rather the definitions emerge from the mappings, which are worked out on the basis of the information provided by the original treebanks. Presumably others could use this initial set of mappings as a guide for how to create new mappings.[7] Regarding the question of whether such a part of speech tagset could be useful for at least some practical applications,

---

[5]Schachter and Shopen [2007] propose the class of interjections as a closed class found in all languages.
[6]More flippantly: 'particle' is the technical term for 'we don't know what the hell this is'; see also Zwicky 1985a.
[7]This might be especially tricky in the case of the category PRT, for 'particles', given the way this term is used in general; see above.

Petrov *et al.* [2012] report promising results in initial experiments on grammar induction and parser transfer.

#50 Part of speech extends to phrasal constituents.

Typological work on part of speech as well as computational work on part of speech tagging considers part of speech at the word level. Both syntactic theories and treebanking efforts, however, also assign tags to phrasal constituents. These tags (or in some cases, complex feature structures) typically reflect information about the part of speech of a distinguished element within the phrase. Thus a noun phrase like *the elephant* is 'nouny' because it has a noun inside of it. Similarly, verb phases like *sleeps*, *eats tomatoes*, or *bets Kim $5 that Sandy will win* are 'verby' because they have verbs inside of them. Some more fine-grained distinctions are also projected to the phrasal level: *the elephants* is a plural noun phrase, because *elephants* is a plural noun. Others are not: the verb phrases *sleeps*, *eats tomatoes*, and *bets Kim $5 that Sandy will win* have the same combinatoric potential, even though the verbs down inside of them belong to different subclasses (based on the arguments they expect within the VP). These topics will be taken up below in #51 on phrases and #52 on heads.

CHAPTER 7

Heads, arguments and adjuncts

#51 Words within sentences form intermediate groupings called constituents.

The words in a sentence are not simply related to each other as elements in a list. Rather, they are organized into groupings, called *constituents*, which then relate to other words in the sentence as a unit. Such structure is made explicit in constituent structure representations such as that of the Penn Treebank [Marcus *et al.*, 1993], but is also implicit in dependency representations, such as that used in the Prague Dependency Treebank [Hajič *et al.*, 2000]. This is illustrated in Figure 7.1, which shows three different structures for the same example. Figure 7.1a gives the Penn Treebank representation, Figure 7.1b the constituent structure assigned by the English Resource Grammar [ERG; Flickinger 2000, 2011], and Figure 7.1c the 'analytical layer' of the Prague Dependency Treebank annotation.[1]

While the two constituent structures (Figure 7.1a and b) are not the same, they do agree that *Dick* and *Darmin* form a constituent, as do *your* and *office* and *call* and *your office*. The dependency structure in Figure 7.1c reflects two of these three constituents: *Dick* is shown as a dependent of *Darmin*, which then relates to the rest of the structure (as the subject of the verb); similarly, *your* is a dependent of *office*. In the dependency structure, however, there is no equivalent of the VP constituent *call your office*, seen in the other two representations.

Constituent structures can be validated by constituency tests. These include coordination (each coordinand being assumed to be a constituent), specific positions within sentences, such as pre-subject position in English, and substitutability of a phrase by a single word. These are illustrated in (57a–c) respectively, where the constituents in question are set off by square brackets:[2]

(57) a. Kim [read a book], [gave it to Sandy], and [left].

b. You said I should read the book and [read it] I did.

c. Kim read [a very interesting book about grammar]./Kim read [it].

---

[1]Figure 7.1a and c are adapted from `http://ufal.mff.cuni.cz/pcedt2.0/`; Figure 7.1b from the output of the ERG demo at `http://erg.delph-in.net`, both accessed on 9/6/12.

[2]These tests are phrased in an English-specific way and illustrated with English-specific examples.

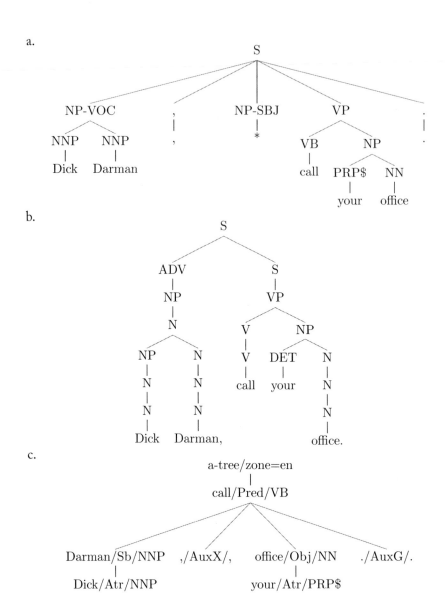

Figure 7.1: Dependency and constituency structures, from: (a) the Penn Treebank, (b) the English Resource Grammar and (c) the Prague Dependency Treebank

It is important to note, however no constituency tests are absolute and in fact it is not uncommon to find counter-examples [see Phillips 2003]. Furthermore, it is impractical to develop and deploy tests like this to motivate every constituency annotation in a large-scale treebanking project or every constituency decision in the development of a broad-coverage grammar. Accordingly, it is quite common to find differences at the level of constituency when comparing across annotation schemes and frameworks. Even in the simple example in Figure 7.1, there are several differences: (i) The treatment of punctuation, attached 'high' (under S) by the PTB and low (as part of the words) by the ERG. (ii) The treatment of the unrealized subject of the imperative *call your office*. In the PTB scheme, this is given a constituent which is a sister to both the vocative NP (*Dick Darman*) and the imperative VP (*call your office*); in the ERG analysis, there is an S constituent with a single daughter (VP). (iii) In addition, the ERG posits many more non-branching constituents. These constituents each represent a phrase structure rule which encodes syntactic and semantic properties only partially represented in the simplified node labels shown in Figure 7.1.

It is clear that constituent structures in any practical project represent many analytical decisions in addition to linguistic properties of the underlying data (not to mention the unavoidable noise introduced in any annotation process). This does not mean that constituent structure treebanks are not useful, but it does mean that they should not be taken as ground truth. In general, constituent structure reflects the ways in which *heads* and *dependents* are combined at a syntactic level to form a scaffolding for the construction of semantic relationships. In addition, constraints on constituent structure, especially on the ordering of constituents with respect to each other and on what is required for a constituent to be complete (see #52) are important to grammaticality. While languages can differ in the rigidity of their word order and the extent to which constituent structure is used to indicate grammatical function (see #78–#80), even the most radically free word order languages still have some evidence for constituents between the level of the word and the whole sentence.

#52 A syntactic head determines the internal structure and external distribution of the constituent it projects.

Within most constituents, there is one distinguished element which is called the *head*.[3] The concept of head (and its relationships to arguments and adjuncts (#53)) is important for understanding the kinds of structures involved in syntax. Identifying heads can also be directly relevant to NLP tasks, for example identifying *camera* as the head of the NP *some good cameras for close ups that are under 200$* is important for recognizing that the whole NP refers to a kind of camera.

The head of a constituent is that sub-constituent which determines the internal structure and external distribution of the constituent as a whole. Thus, for example, in (58a), the constituent

---

[3]Only most, and not all, constituents because there are cases where no unique head can be identified. A clear example here is coordination: the conjunction does not qualify as a head in *Kim slept and Sandy read.*.

give Sandy books has *give* as its head. The remaining two parts of the constituent, *Sandy* and *books* are licensed to be there because *give* is the kind of verb that requires two complements (semantically, a recipient and a theme; syntactically an indirect object NP and a direct object NP, in this use of *give*). It is a further property of the verb *give* that one of these arguments is obligatory, but not the other, as shown in (58b–c) (see #55). As illustrated by the unacceptability of (58d), the verb *see* does not provide for two complements in this way. Externally, because *give* is a verb (and furthermore a non-finite/untensed form of the verb), the whole constituent can appear in positions expecting such verbal constituents, such as after the modal *would* (58e) and as the second complement of *helped* (58f). By the same token, *give Sandy books* cannot appear in positions that are not expecting verbal constituents of this type, such as subject position (58g).

(58)   a. Kim planned to give Sandy books.

       b. *Kim planned to give Sandy.

       c. Kim planned to give books.

       d. *Kim planned to see Sandy books.

       e. Kim would give Sandy books.

       f. Pat helped Kim give Sandy books.

       g. *Give Sandy books surprised Kim.

A similar set of examples concerning a noun functioning as a head is given in (59). The contrast between (59a) and (59b) shows that *war* provides for different internal structure in the NP it is the head of than *battle* does.[4] The contrast between (59c) and (59d) illustrates the way in which the head determines the external distribution of the NP. Here the agreement with the main verb depends on the number head of the NP (*war*) and not the number of the other noun (*drugs/addiction*), which is not the head of the larger NP.

(59)   a. The war on drugs is controversial.

       b. *The battle on drugs is controversial.

       c. The war on drugs/addiction is controversial.

       d. *The war on drugs/addiction are controversial.

The notion that a head 'projects' a domain in which it controls the dependents that appear and the overall character of the resulting constituent is at the core of many theoretical approaches to syntax, including X-Bar Theory [e.g., Emonds 1976, see also Kornai and Pullum 1990] and Head-driven Phrase Structure Grammar [HPSG; Pollard and Sag 1994].

While there is in general more agreement about headedness than about the details of constituent structure, there are still some cases which are unclear, and which thus are characterized by disagreements in the literature. A case in point is the combination of a determiner and a noun,

---

[4]Implicit in this argumentation is the claim that *on drugs* is functioning as a argument rather than an adjunct, see #53.

which some theories treat as an NP (i.e., headed by the noun) and others as a DP (i.e., headed by the determiner). See Zwicky 1985b for an insightful discussion of the bundle of properties ascribed to syntactic heads and how they do and don't correlate.

#53 Syntactic dependents can be classified as arguments and adjuncts.

Within any given headed constituent,[5] subconstituents which are not the head are *dependents*. Dependents come in two types: *Arguments* are dependents which are syntactically selected or licensed by the head and typically complete the meaning of a predicate. *Adjuncts* are dependents which do not need to be licensed and are not selected for by the head and which refine the meaning of a complete predication [Kay, 2005]. These notions are closely related to the distinction between *core* frame elements in FrameNet on the one hand and *peripheral* and *extra-thematic* ones on the other [Fillmore and Baker, 2004].

While these distinctions may seem clear in principle, in practice there are many cases which can be difficult to decide. For one thing, the syntactic and semantic characterizations do not always correlate and are not always applicable. The remainder of this chapter provides an overview of properties of arguments and adjuncts, many of which can be operationalized as tests. Perhaps more importantly, these properties provide further information about the ways in which dependents relate to heads, which should be useful in the development of NLP systems which use information about constituent structure or dependency structure as input to additional tasks.

#54–#56 concern the notion of semantic arguments and their relationship to semantic predicates on the one hand and syntactic arguments on the other. #57 and #58 explore syntactic and semantic properties of adjuncts, which lead to tests for the argument/adjunct status described in #59 and #60. #61–#64 provide examples of various kinds of adjuncts. Finally, #66 and #67 discuss what determines whether a constituent can be an adjunct or an argument, in general.

#54 The number of semantic arguments provided for by a head is a fundamental lexical property.

A lexical item is a pairing of form and meaning [de Saussure, 1916]. The form side of this consists of the phonological form of the stem as well as any information required to handle morphologically conditioned allomorphy (see #25) and information about the syntax (part of speech, syntactic argument structure) of the word. The meaning side minimally consists of a predicate symbol and a list of arguments expected for that predicate.[6] The mapping of forms to meanings is not one-to-one, but rather many-to-many. That is, the same form can be linked (in different lexical entries) to different meanings (homophones) and vice versa (synonyms). Given a

---

[5]See note 3, page 63
[6]More fine-grained meaning representations are possible, given the results of studies in lexical semantics, e.g., Pustejovsky 1991. Even so, such representations should include a list of argument positions.

specific lexical entry (form-pairing meaning), however, there is a specific semantic predicate with its associated list of argument positions.[7]

Given a comprehensive lexicon listing the kind of form-meaning pairings described here, determining the arguments expected by a lexical item in running text would be a matter of disambiguation.[8] Of course, creating such a lexicon is an extraordinarily difficult task, but one on which the FrameNet project[9] (Baker *et al.* 1998) has made an impressive start.[10] Practically speaking, such a resource can never be complete. Nonetheless, it is useful to understand lexical predicates as seeking specific numbers of arguments and encoding specific roles for each argument, even if we do not know what these are in a given case. This contrasts with adjuncts, discussed below, which are not lexically anticipated by the head.

#55 In many (perhaps all) languages, (some) arguments can be left unexpressed.

While the number of semantic arguments anticipated by a head is established by its lexical entry (and any relevant morphological processes), not all of these arguments are necessarily always overtly expressed. This is illustrated in (60), which gives examples taken from the FrameNet database.[11] (60a) has explicit representation of the core frame elements Speaker (*I*), Message (*You are on the mend*) and Addressee (*you*).[12] In (60b), the Speaker (*He*) and Message (*that … break*) are expressed, but the Addressee is left implicit. In (60c), the Speaker is implicit, but the Addressee (*Parents*) and Message (*the right … times*) are overt.[13]

(60)   a. You are on the mend, I promise you.

     b. He promised that the Clinton administration would make a clean break.

     c. Parents have been promised the right to stay in hospital with their sick children at all times.

Argument 'drop' is discussed further in #96 and #97. For now, it is important to note two things: First, the lexical entry indicates which arguments are expected, even if they are not overtly expressed. Unexpressed semantic arguments are still semantically present, and thus detecting them can be important for coreference resolution as well as natural language understanding more generally. Second, the fact that at least some arguments are only optionally expressed means that optionality is not a sufficient condition for adjunct status, see #59.

[7]Not all linguists take this point of view. See Goldberg 1995 and Haugereid 2004 for discussion and Kay 2005 for counterpoint.
[8]The picture is slightly complicated by lexical processes that can alter the expected semantic arguments of a lexical item. A case in point is causative constructions, discussed in #87.
[9]https://framenet.icsi.berkeley.edu
[10]There is also work on machine learning approaches to extending such resources, through deep lexical acquisition [e.g., Baldwin 2005, Moschitti and Basili 2005, Zhang and Kordoni 2006].
[11]https://framenet2.icsi.berkeley.edu/fnReports/data/lu/lu481.xml?mode=annotation, accessed on 9/6/12
[12]FrameNet also lists Topic and Medium as core FEs.
[13]There are no examples annotated where the Message is unexpressed, but such examples are easy to create: *But you promised!*

Finally, note that the boundary between argument optionality and homophony is not always clear. It is a matter of long-standing debate in linguistics [see Levin 1993, 33] whether both of the examples in (61) involve the same lexical entry for *eat*, with an optional argument, or if there are two verbs *eat*, one of which is obligatorily transitive and the other obligatorily intransitive.

(61)   a.   Kim ate dinner.

        b.   Kim ate.

#56 Words from different parts of speech can serve as heads selecting arguments

While work on argument structure often focuses on verbs, in fact many different parts of speech can serve as heads selecting arguments. (62) gives examples of nouns taking arguments:

(62)   a.   Kim's *invitation* of the media to the event surprised everyone.

        b.   The *invitation* by Kim of the media to the even surprised everyone.

        c.   Sandy's *arrival* was earlier than expected.

        d.   The early *arrival* by Sandy threw off the schedule.

In these examples, the nouns are derived from verbs. The realization of the arguments of such *deverbal* nouns is systematically related to the realization of the arguments of the verbs they are derived from [Chomsky, 1970]. Note that the position to the left of the noun (sometimes called the *specifier* position) sometimes has a semantic argument (*Kim's* and *Sandy's* in (62a,c)) and sometimes instead houses a determiner which does not fill a semantic argument position of the noun. Nonetheless, the determiner is still treated as a syntactic dependent of the noun.[14]

Argument-taking nouns don't have to be deverbal. We also find nouns that are not derived from other stems taking arguments (beyond the determiner) as well as nouns derived from adjectives taking arguments:

(63)   a.   The *recipe* for the winning pie was never revealed.

        b.   The *fact* that the pie won was undisputed.

        c.   The *likelihood* of Sandy being on time is low.

        d.   Kim's *unhappiness* about the surprise was understandable.

Both the NomBank [Meyers *et al.*, 2004] and FrameNet [Baker *et al.*, 1998] projects have annotated argument frames for nouns.

(64) gives some examples of adjectives selecting arguments:

---

[14]The headedness of constituents like *Kim's book* or *the invitation by Kim of the media to the event* is actually a point of disagreement in the syntactic literature, with some authors treating these constituents as DPs headed by the determiner and others treating them as NPs headed by the noun (see #52). Even when the constituent is considered an NP, with the determiner as syntactic dependent of the noun, the noun may be a semantic dependent of the determiner.

(64)   a. Kim is *proud* of that painting.

b. Sandy is *unhappy* about the weather.

c. Pat is *likely* to arrive late.

d. Chris is *surprised* that the kids laughed.

It is worth noting here that just like nouns and verbs, adjectives take a range of types of constituents as arguments. The examples above illustrate PPs (64a,b), infinitival clauses (64c), and finite clauses (64d). In addition, semantically, the subject is functioning as a semantic argument of the adjective in (64a,b,d) (see #90 on how this connection is made[15]).

Adpositions also take arguments. Syntactically, only one constituent is typically directly attached as an argument. The other semantic position can be filled by the head that the PP attaches to as an adjunct (see #58) or via raising (see #90). Examples of adpositions taking arguments are shown in (65). Most English adpositions are prepositions, so the syntactic argument shows up to the right. Example (65d) shows an exceptional postposition; its syntactic argument is to its left.

(65)   a. Sandy found the light switch *above* the counter.

b. Kim watched the movie *before* it was released.

c. The guests at the surprise party jumped *out from behind* the couch.

d. The show was supposed to have started fifteen minutes *ago*.

As with the other parts of speech, prepositions can take a range of syntactic categories as arguments. The examples in (65) illustrate NP (*the counter, the couch, fifteen minutes*), S (*it was released*) and PP (*behind the couch, from behind the couch*) arguments.

Across all parts of speech, the specific number and type of constituents that are selected depend on the selecting head. Thus even though some verbs can take clauses marked by *that* as complements, some nouns can take *of* PPs, some adjectives can take *to*-marked infinitival clauses and some adpositions can take PPs arguments, the examples in (66), not all of them can, as shown by the ungrammatical examples in (66).

(66)   a. Kim *knows* that pizza is yummy.

b. *Kim *ate* that pizza is yummy.

c. Kim's *collection* of ideas was intriguing.

d. *Kim's *cat* of ideas was intriguing.

e. Kim is *ready* to make pizza.

f. *Kim is *lazy* to make pizza.

g. Kim found the light switch *down* behind the counter.

h. *Kim found the light switch *above* behind the counter.

[15]In (64c) *likely* doesn't have a semantic role for the subject, but otherwise the structures are analogous.

#57 Adjuncts are not required by heads and generally can iterate.

In contrast to arguments, adjuncts are not selected or licensed by the heads they combine with. Rather, they appear 'freely', that is, can be added to any constituent of the appropriate type. The adjuncts themselves specify which type — syntactic and semantic — of constituent they can combine with, see #62–#64 and #66. Thus any adjunct that can modify the appropriate semantic type of VP can appear as a modifier of *ran, ate pizza,* or *sent letters to Kim*:

(67)   a.   Sandy ran in Berlin/on Saturday/with friends.

     b.   Kim ate pizza in Berlin/on Saturday/with friends.

     c.   Pat sent letters to Kim in Berlin/on Saturday/with friends.

When an adjunct attaches to a head, the resulting constituent generally shares the syntactic properties of the head. As a consequence, adjuncts can generally iterate, as illustrated in the following examples with six temporal adjuncts and two manner adjuncts, respectively:

(68)   a.   They arrived [in September] [on the last Saturday] [in the afternoon] [around 3pm] [five minutes before the end of the game] [before anyone left].

     b.   They decorated the cake [with great care] [using fondant].

This contrasts with arguments, which cannot iterate. That is, each argument position can be filled by only one argument, though that argument may be coordinated:

(69)   a.   Kim gave Sandy a book.

     b.   *Kim gave Sandy a book a record.

     c.   Kim gave Sandy a book and a record.

Note, however, that in some languages, coordination is achieved through simple juxtaposition (see #93), as in the example in (70) from Awtuw, a language of Papua New Guinea [Feldman, 1986, 67]:

(70)   Yowmen Yawur du-k-puy-ey
     Yomen   Yawur   DUR-IMPF-hit-IMPF

     'Yowmen and Yawur are hitting (someone).' [awt]

This is not interpreted as the verb having two subjects, but rather the verb having one, coordinated subject. Stassen [2011] notes that while this kind of coordination is fairly common in the world's languages, it is rare for it to be the only way for a language to coordinate NPs.

#58 Adjuncts are syntactically dependents but semantically introduce predicates with take the syntactic head as an argument.

Within a headed constituent, there is one head; all other sub-constituents are dependents. Despite the fact that adjuncts are not selected, they are still dependents, because it can be shown that another element must be the head. The key observation here is that in an example like (71a), the modified VP *ate the pizza in a hurry* has the same combinatoric potential as the unmodified VP *ate the pizza* within it. That is, it can appear in environments which expect a finite VP and not in environments that don't. Thus the smaller VP *ate the pizza* is analyzed as the head of the larger VP *ate the pizza in a hurry*.

(71)   a.   Kim ate the pizza in a hurry.

     b.   *Kim did ate the pizza.

     c.   *Kim did ate the pizza in a hurry.

     d.   Kim ran home and ate the pizza.

     e.   Kim ran home and ate the pizza in a hurry.

However, adjuncts present a case in which the direction of the syntactic and semantic dependencies differ: Despite being syntactic dependents, adjuncts semantically function to introduce predicates which take the constituent they modify as an argument. The sentence in (72) describes a barking situation in which the dog is the barker and a state of affairs in which something—the barking—was loud.

(72)   The dog barked loudly.

Just as syntactic heads can place constraints (both hard and soft) on the semantic type of their arguments, adjuncts can place constraints (both hard and soft) on the semantic type of the heads they combine with. This is illustrated in (73), which illustrates how adjuncts like *in an hour* typically combine with VPs describing events with an inherent endpoint while adjuncts like *for an hour* typically combine with VPs describing events without an inherent endpoint.[16,17]

(73)   a.   Kim ate a whole pizza in an hour.

     b.   ?Kim ate a whole pizza for an hour.

     c.   ?Kim ate pizza in an hour.

     d.   Kim ate pizza for an hour.

All adjuncts have this property of functioning as semantic heads. On the other hand, while most arguments are semantic (as well as syntactic) dependents, there are cases of arguments which are not semantic dependents. For one thing, there are syntactic heads which are semantically empty (see #88), and thus have no argument positions to fill as well as those which select more syntactic than semantic arguments (see #90). Beyond that, there are cases in which it appears an element is syntactically required by a head but the desired semantic representation looks more like that of an adjunct. (74) shows two examples based on analyses from the ERG [Flickinger,

---

[16]This contrast is one of *telicity*, where *eat a whole pizza* is *telic* while *eat pizza* is *atelic*.

[17](73b) and (73c) are marked with ? rather than * to indicate degraded acceptability but not outright unacceptability. See note 5 on page 4.

2000, 2011]. In (74a), *too badly* is syntactically selected by the verb *do* but semantically takes *do* as an argument. In (74b), *very well* is syntactically selected as the second argument of *put*, but analyzed again as a semantic modifier of the verb.

(74)　a.　I'm not doing too badly.

　　　b.　You put it very well.

#59 Obligatoriness can be used as a test to distinguish arguments from adjuncts.

It follows from the facts that arguments are selected (#52) and adjuncts occur freely (#57) that obligatoriness can be used as a diagnostic test in some cases where it's not clear whether a dependent is an argument or an adjunct. If omitting the element leads to an ungrammatical string, then it must be selected, i.e., an argument. The converse, however, is not true: as discussed above (#55), some arguments are optional, and so optionality does not establish adjunct status.

In English, locative PPs are notoriously tricky to classify as arguments or adjuncts. The obligatoriness test shows that the verb *put* selects for a PP argument:[18]

(75)　a.　Kim put the pen in the drawer.

　　　b.　*Kim put the pen.

#60 Entailment can be used as a test to distinguish arguments from adjuncts.

Another difference between arguments and adjuncts which can be turned into a diagnostic test turns on the semantic independence of adjuncts. Because adjuncts introduce predicates which take the elements they modify as arguments, that relationship will stay the same if modified element is replaced with a more general pro-form [Hawkins, 2000]. Thus (76a) entails (76b) and (76c) entails (76d):

(76)　a.　Pat slept until noon.

　　　b.　Pat did something until noon.

　　　c.　Pat ate lunch in Montreal.

　　　d.　Pat did something in Montreal.

If, however, the element in question is an argument and not a modifier, switching out the verb will not result in the same entailment relations. Contrast the examples in (77) with those in (76). Here (77a) and (77c) do not entail (77b) and (77d).

---

[18]Modeling this kind of information can be directly useful in reducing ambiguity (and thus simplifying the task of disambiguation). That is, a parser that knows that *put* requires a PP complement would not propose an analysis for (75a) where the PP attaches to the noun *pen* instead of to the verb.

(77)   a. Pat relied on Chris.

     b. Pat did something on Chris.

     c. Pat put nuts in a cup.

     d. Pat did something in a cup.

This is evidence that *rely* and *put* select for PP complements. That conclusion is further supported by the obligatoriness test (#59), as shown in (78):

(78)   a. *Pat relied.

     b. *Pat put nuts.

In the case of *rely* there is one further piece of evidence that the PP is selected: Only PPs headed by *on* (or somewhat archaically, *upon*) will do.

(79)   *Pat relied near/above/in/for Chris.

#61 Adjuncts can be single words, phrases, or clauses.

A constituent functioning as an adjunct can have a variety of different internal structures, ranging from single words (80), to phrases (81), to whole clauses (82).[19]

(80)   a. Kim went sailing *yesterday*.

     b. The boat had a *blue* sail.

     c. The trip was *very* long.

(81)   a. Sandy read a book *on the bus*.

     b. The book has a *very elaborate* plot line.

     c. The book was just released *the day before yesterday*.

(82)   a. Sandy kept reading the book *while the bus was stuck in traffic*.

     b. The book was engrossing *because the plot was so complicated*.

     c. *If the bus drove off the road*, Sandy might not even have noticed.

     d. The book was written by an author *whose work Sandy had not read before*.

Inside each of the phrasal and clausal modifiers, there is a word or syntactic construction involved which confers the potential to function as an adjunct to the phrase or clause (see #66). In (81a,b), the words in question are *on* and *elaborate*; in (82a–c) they are *while, because* and *if*.[20]

---

[19]Clauses are a subset of phrases, specifically those that include a predicative element (typically a verb) and all of its arguments. Clauses may also include modifiers.

[20]When a single word is responsible for the ability of a phrase to function as an adjunct, it is always the syntactic head of that phrase.

The ERG's [Flickinger, 2000, 2011] analyses of (81c) and (82d) involve special syntactic rules. In the former, it is a rule which creates an adverbial modifier out of the NP *the day before yesterday*. In the latter, the rule in question licenses the combination of *whose book* and *Sandy had not read before* to create the relative clause.

#62 Adjuncts can modify nominal constituents.

Just as heads of different categories can select for arguments, heads of different categories can also be modified by adjuncts. Adjuncts modifying nouns and constituents projected from nouns are called *adnominal modifiers*, a class which (in English) includes adjectives (83a), adjective phrases (83b), adpositional phrases (PPs) (83c), and relative clauses (83d) as well as appositive NPs (83e) and others.[21]

(83) a. The *blue* car went by fast.

b. Anyone *unhappy about their assignment* should contact HR.

c. The cat *on the mat* looks content.

d. The plant *which Kim planted to the right of the door* is thriving.

e. That plant, *the one Sandy planted*, is not doing as well.

#63 Adjuncts can modify verbal constituents.

Adjuncts modifying verbs and constituents projected from verbs are called *adverbial modifiers*. In English, these include adverbs (84a), adpositional phrases (PPs) (84b), certain temporal noun phrases (84c), subordinate clauses (84d), discourse markers (84e), and others.

(84) a. Kim runs *quickly*.

b. Kim ran the race *in under 20 minutes*.

c. Kim runs races *every other weekend*.

d. Kim started running, *not realizing the starting gun hadn't gone off*.

e. *Well*, it was an honest mistake.

[21]It is a quirk of English syntax that when adjectives appear as single-word modifiers of nouns they attach to the left, while adjective phrases modifying nouns attach to the right. Other quirks appear in other languages: the Romance languages, for example, have a lexical class of adjectives which appear to the left of nouns they modify where most adjectives appears to the right, as illustrated for French in (i):

(i) a. Le   *jeune*   chat est   mignon.
        The.SG.M young.SG.M cat.SG be.PRES.3SG cute.SG.M

    'The young cat is cute.' [fra]

b. Le   chat *noir*   est   mignon.
        The.SG.M cat.SG black.SG.M be.PRES.3SG cute.SG.M

    'The black cat is cute.' [fra]

#64 Adjuncts can modify other types of constituents.

Not just nominal and verbal constituents but other types of constituents can take adjuncts as well. In English, we find adverbs modifying adjectives (85a), adverbs modifying PPs (85b), degree modifiers modifying adverbs (85c,d)[22] and even adverbs modifying determiners (85e).

(85)   a.   The *surprisingly* anxious crowd was starting to worry Sandy.

b.   The best seats were *right* at the front.

c.   The crowd dispersed *very* quickly.

d.   The crowd dispersed *more* quickly than we expected it to.

e.   *Almost* every spectator left.

#65 Adjuncts express a wide range of meanings.

Adjuncts can be classified based on the type of meaning they add to the constituent they attach to. Probably the best way to get a sense of the range of these meanings is to look at the categories developed in large-scale annotation projects. Table 7.1 gives the types of modifiers of verbal projections listed in the PropBank [Kingsbury and Palmer, 2002] annotation guidelines [Babko-Malaya, 2005].[23] The PropBank guidelines also have a catch-all category called 'Adverbials' for modifiers that don't fit the other categories. 'Adverbials' include modifiers like *probably*, *fortunately*, *only*, *even*, *except for* and a variety of others.[24]

#66 The potential to be a modifier is inherent to the syntax of a constituent.

The tests for distinguishing adjuncts from arguments discussed briefly in #59 and #60 are applicable to constituents in context. This is because one and the same phrase can function as an adjunct in one context and an argument in another. For example, in (86a), *in the box* is an argument while in (86b) and (86c) it is an adjunct:

(86)   a.   Kim put the books in the box.

b.   Sandy saw the books in the box.

c.   The books in the box were all original editions.

---

[22]The construction in (85d) is a rather complicated one where *than we expected it to* is actually a dependent of *more* [Huddleston and Pullum, 2002, 1104].

[23]Examples given here are shortened versions of those in Babko-Malaya 2005, where available. The names for the modifier types are also shortened. The term 'reciprocal' is used in an unusual fashion here, to cover uses of words like *himself* as well as *each other*, *jointly*, *both* as adjuncts to verbal projections.

[24]The PropBank guidelines also consider modals (*must*, *might* etc.), but in fact these are not syntactically adjuncts.

Table 7.1: Verbal projection modifier types in PropBank

Type	Example
Directional	Workers dumped the material *into a huge bin*.
Locative	Areas of the factory were dusty *where the crocidolite was used*.
Manner	Workers *mechanically* mixed the dry fibers.
Temporal	Asbestos caused a high percentage of cancer deaths among workers exposed to it *more than 30 years ago*.
Extent	Shares closed yesterday at $3.75, *off 25 cents*.
Reciprocal	The stadium was such a good idea someone would build it *himself*.
Secondary predicate	Pierre Vinken will join the board *as a nonexecutive director*.
Purpose clause	Commonwealth Edison could raise its electricity rates *to pay for the plant*.
Cause clause	Five other countries will remain on the watch list *as a result of an interim review*.
Discourse marker	*But* for now, they're looking forward to their winter meeting.
Negation	Kim *no longer* works here.

Whether a particular word or phrase can function as an adjunct, and if so, which kind of constituents it can modify, are inherent properties of that phrase. For example, most English PPs can modify either nominal or verbal heads, but PPs headed by *of* generally do not modify verbal heads [Huddleston and Pullum, 2002, 659]:

(87)　a.　The reactions *after the event* were strong.

　　　b.　Kim arrived *after the event*.

　　　c.　The garden *over the wall* is quiet and peaceful.

　　　d.　Kim stared *over the wall*.

　　　e.　The first flowers *of Spring* are always a welcome sight.

　　　f.　*The flowers bloomed *of Spring*.

The fact that the adjuncts themselves determine what they can modify is related to their ability to iterate and more generally to attach freely to any constituent of they type they modify (see #57).

#67 Just about anything can be an argument, for some head.

The most canonical arguments are NPs and PPs, followed by clauses. However, just about any constituent can function as an argument, for the right head: As noted in #52, on some analyses at least, determiners are arguments of nouns (88a). Certain English verbs select for adverbs as complements (88b,c).

(88)   a. Kim read *a* book.

b. That doesn't bode *well*.

c. *That doesn't bode.

English verb-particle constructions involve verbs selecting for specific 'particles' which are homophonous with prepositions but don't take complements themselves. That is, the verb selects the 'particle' (here *up*) as a single-word complement rather than a PP. This is particularly clear in examples where the particle is the final word in the sentence:

(89)   Let's look it up.

The counterpart of this construction in Dutch and related languages is separable-prefix verbs, where in some cases the 'particle' appears as part of the verb (orthographically, at least) and in others it is a separate argument [Booij, 1990, 46]:[25]

(90)   a. John belde   me   op
John bel-de   me   op
John call-PST.SG 1SG.ACC up

'John phoned me.' [nld]

b. dat John me   wil   opbellen.
dat John me   wil   op-bel-en.
that John 1SG.ACC want.PRES.SG up-call.INF

'that John wants to phone me.' [nld]

Another unlikely-seeming argument type is number names. In languages such as Japanese, Chinese, Thai and others, number names must combine with numeral classifiers in order to modify nouns. On the analysis of Bender and Siegel [2004], the numeral classifier is treated as the head of the number name-numeral classifier construction, selecting the number name as an argument. An example from Japanese is shown in (91).

(91)   猫   二 匹   を 飼う。
Neko ni hiki   wo kau.
cat   2 NUMCL ACC raise

'(I) am raising two cats.' [jpn] [Bender and Siegel, 2004]

Given that just about anything can be an adjunct (in the right context) and just about anything can be an argument (in the right context), one might wonder if it's worthwhile attempting

---

[25]In both the Englishand Dutch cases, the 'particle' is arguably only a syntactic, and not a semantic, argument. On such an analysis, the verb contributes the meaning associated with the verb-particle pair and idiosyncratically selects for a semantically empty particle of the right form.

to make the distinction at all. To the extent that accurate semantic representations bring value to NLP applications, it is, as the direction of semantic dependencies is affected by the argument or adjunct status of a syntactic dependent. Among other things, that can affect the entailments of a sentence (see #60 and Hawkins 2000). Even applications that don't require deep semantic representations can benefit from distinguishing between arguments and adjuncts in running text and building lexical resources which model the argument requirements of heads, because these distinctions can potentially help with ambiguity resolution and approximations of lexical semantics.

Though there is a wide range of lexical variation and lexical detail here, it is not a lost cause. Especially for well-described languages, there are rich linguistic resources available which do draw the distinction between arguments and adjuncts, including annotated resources like PropBank [Kingsbury and Palmer, 2002] and FrameNet [Baker *et al.*, 1998] and grammars like the ERG [Flickinger, 2000, 2011].

CHAPTER 8

Argument types and grammatical functions

#68 There is no agreed upon universal set of semantic roles, even for one language; nonetheless, arguments can be roughly categorized semantically.

For many years, linguists sought to express generalizations in terms of *semantic roles* which apply across verbs and across languages (e.g., Chomsky 1981, Fillmore 1968, Gruber 1965, Jackendoff 1972).[1] Lists of such so-called 'thematic roles' or 'theta-roles' typically start with the following:[2]

- Agent: A participant which the meaning of the verb specifies as doing or causing something, possibly intentionally. *Examples:* subjects of *kill, eat, hit, smash, kick, watch*.

- Patient: A participant which the verb characterizes as having something happen to it, and as being affected by what happens to it. *Examples:* objects of *kill, eat, smash* but not those of *watch, hear* and *love*.

- Experiencer: A participant who is characterized as aware of something. *Examples:* subject of *love*, object of *annoy*.

- Theme: A participant which is characterized as changing its position or condition, or as being in a state or position. *Examples:* objects of *give, hand*, subjects of *walk, die*.

One semantic function of thematic roles is supposed to be to characterize and differentiate between the ways in which arguments relate to a predicate. Clearly, the sentence *Kim eats pizza.* describes an event in which Kim and the pizza participate in very different ways. It seems equally clear that this differentiated participation is part of the meaning of the verb *eat*.[3] Where the difficulty arises is in drawing analogies across different verbs. As Dowty [1991] points out, no one has ever proposed a comprehensive set of thematic roles for any single language nor a rigorous set

---

[1]In fact, Dowty [1989] identifies Pāṇini's 6th century BCE concept of *kārakas* as an instance of this idea.

[2]Definitions from Dowty 1989 after Andrews 1985.

[3]Though as Dowty [1991] notes there are verbs which have more than one argument which participate in the same way in the event or situation they describe, for example: *x resembles y*.

of operationalizable definitions.[4] If there is no set that applies comprehensively and systematically within one language, *a fortiori*, there cannot be a single cross-linguistic set, either.

However, the semantic role characterizing function of thematic roles does not require the same roles to apply across different predicates. Thus many authors [e.g., Marantz 1984, Sag *et al.* 2003, van Riemsdijk and Williams 1986] opt to define specific thematic roles for each predicate (such that *read* takes 'reader' and 'reading material' arguments, rather than agent and theme). Even projects that reuse role names across predicates, such as the English Resource Grammar [ERG; Flickinger 2000, 2011] or PropBank [Kingsbury and Palmer, 2002], now typically stipulate that there is room for variation in the interpretation of the role names across predicates [Flickinger *et al.*, 2005, Palmer *et al.*, 2005]. Dowty [1991], however, suggests that this is perhaps going too far, and that generalizations can be drawn about arguments across verbs so long as the role types are viewed as prototypes (specifically, Proto-Agent and Proto-Patient) such that specific roles for specific verbs might have only some subset of the properties associated with the relevant proto-role.

#69 Arguments can also be categorized syntactically, though again there may not be universal syntactic argument types.

Whereas semantic roles are not necessarily generalizable across predicates, there are syntactic roles (also called 'grammatical functions') which can be applied across predicates, at least within languages.[5] Again, the best way to get a sense of the range of argument types is to look at projects which have achieved broad-coverage over linguistic data.

Some of the Penn Treebank [Marcus *et al.*, 1993] function tags indicate a small range of grammatical argument types:[6]

- -SBJ: the surface subject in any clause
  (NP-SBJ *John*) *put the book on the table.*

- -LGS: the NP corresponding to the 'logical subject' of passives (see #84)
  That was painted by (NP-LGS *Mark*).

- -DTV: PP marking the so-called 'dative' argument of a three argument verb
  I asked a question (PP-DTV *of the president*).

- -PUT: the locative argument of *put*
  John put the book (PP-PUT *on the table*).

[4]Dowty [1991] cites Blake [1930] as having made the most progress towards a comprehensive set. Blake's proposal included 113 roles.

[5]There is some disagreement among grammatical theories as to whether grammatical functions are best treated as primitives of the theory or as notions derived from other constructs, such as phrase structural configurations, or even not present at all [Kaplan and Bresnan, 1982, McCloskey, 1997]. However, this controversy is orthogonal to the points raised here: the key point is that syntactic structure is distinct from but linked to semantic structure.

[6]This list is taken from Bies *et al.* 1995.

The Penn Treebank function tags also include tags for functions which do not correspond to grammatical arguments, including -PRD marking non-verbal predicates, and -VOC marking vocative noun phrases (e.g., *Kim* in *Kim, do you know when Sandy left?*). There are many kinds of non-subject arguments that do not receive specific marking in this set (see below). In addition, it is not clear why the verb *put* gets special treatment. The Penn Treebank is primarily concerned with constituent structure and the function tags were added in a separate annotation pass [Bies *et al.*, 1995, 35]. Furthermore, many grammatical functions in English can be uniquely identified by phrase structural notions. Thus, while the range of function tags for adjuncts is more complete, it is perhaps not surprising that the coverage of grammatical functions in the Treebank is not extensive.

Dependency representations, on the other hand, if they are to include labels, require a comprehensive set of dependency labels. If the dependency relations represented are syntactic (rather than semantic, see Ivanova *et al.* 2012), these labels will include a classification of grammatical argument types. de Marneffe and Manning [2008] [see also de Marneffe and Manning 2011] present a dependency representation scheme which builds on theoretical foundations from Lexical-Functional Grammar [Bresnan, 2001, Kaplan and Bresnan, 1982] and is specifically designed for practical use in NLP. The set of dependency labels includes the labels shown in Table 8.1, which correspond to arguments.[7]

These dependency types are organized into a hierarchy, such that the subject types (nsubj, nsubjpass, csubj, csubjpass) are all considered types of a more general type 'subj', etc. In general, these types express distinctions which involve both the role of the dependent with respect to the head (subject or complement) and the grammatical category of the argument. For example, the distinction between nsubj and csubj is in the grammatical form of the subject (NP v. clause) and the distinction between ccomp and xcomp is in whether the clause functioning as a complement contains its own subject or relies on the larger linguistic structure for the interpretation of the subject (see #90–#91).

Note that de Marneffe and Manning [2008] do not draw a strong distinction between arguments and adjuncts. The dependency types listed above are presented together with non-argument dependency types. Furthermore, there is no separate dependency type for PPs functioning as arguments; they are lumped together with PP adjuncts under the label 'prep'.[8]

A third view on syntactic argument roles is provided by the FrameNet project [Baker *et al.*, 1998]. Ruppenhofer *et al.* [2010] list a very small set of grammatical functions. These are shown in Table 8.2, along with the heads which they are associated. These functions also collapse arguments and adjuncts, as this distinction is drawn in the FrameNet representation at the level of the

---

[7]These descriptions and some of the examples are from de Marneffe and Manning 2011. In these examples, the dependent filling the named argument role is in italics while the selecting head is in boldface. Here the entire constituent filling the argument role is italicized, while a dependency structure would only link to the head of that constituent.

[8]de Marneffe and Manning [2008] describe the argument/adjunct distinction as 'largely useless in practice' (p. 3), but their view might have been influenced by the fact that their training data (the Penn Treebank) doesn't make a clear distinction between arguments and adjuncts. See also Zaenen and Crouch 2009 for a proposal to assimilate a certain class of PP arguments to adjuncts in the ParGram English grammar.

Table 8.1: Argument dependency types from de Marneffe and Manning 2011

Tag	Type	Example
nsubj	nominal subject	*Kim* **took** the picture.
nsubjpass	passive nsubj	*The picture* was **taken** by Kim.
csubj	clausal subject	*What she said* **makes** sense.
csubjpassive	passive csubj	*That she lied* was **suspected** by everyone.
xsubj	controlling subject	*Kim* likes to **take** pictures.
agent	in passives	The picture was **taken** by *Kim*.
expl	existential *there*	*There* **is** a ghost in the room.
dobj	direct object	They **win** *the lottery*.
iobj	indirect object	She **gave** *me* a raise.
ccomp	clausal complement	He **says** *that you like to swim*.
xcomp	controlled clause	You **like** *to swim*.
acomp	adjectival complement	Bill **looks** *very big*.
pcomp	preposition's clausal complement	They heard **about** *you missing class*.
pobj	object of preposition	They sat **on** *the chair*.
prt	phrasal verb particle	They **shut** *down* the station.
cop	complement of copular verb	Bill **is** *big*.
attr	*wh* complement of copular verb	*What* **is** that?

semantic role (frame element) annotations (*Ibid.* p.66). Note also that while head nouns modified by adjectives certainly have a semantic role to play with respect to the semantic predicate of the adjective, the noun is considered the head in the syntactic dependency between the two (see #58).

Table 8.2: FrameNet Grammatical Functions [Ruppenhofer *et al.*, 2010]

Grammatical Function	V	A	P	N
External Argument	✓	✓	✓	✓
Dependent	✓	✓	✓	✓
Object	✓			
Modified head noun		✓		
Genitive determiner				✓
Appositive				✓

Some examples of 'external arguments' of different types of heads are shown in (92), (93) gives examples of the 'dependent' category.[9] The selecting heads are in bold face; the constituents filling the 'external argument' or 'dependent' role are in italics.

(92)　a. *The physician* **performed** the surgery.

　　　b. *The chair* is **red**.

　　　c. *the day* **before** yesterday

　　　d. *He* made a **statement** to the press.

(93)　a. Pat **spoke** *to me*.

　　　b. I **expect** your papers *the moment you walk into class*.

　　　c. Lee is **certain** *of his innocence*.

　　　d. We had a glass of wine **before** *the meal*.

　　　e. a **story** *about a young entrepreneur*

#70 A subject is the distinguished argument of a predicate and may be the only one to display certain grammatical properties.

One thing that emerges from the categorizations of arguments discussed in #69 is that subjects are special. While there is no existing universal classification of syntactic argument types, perhaps the closest the field has come to identifying one type that appears cross-linguistically is with the notion of subject [Keenan, 1976], though even this is highly contentious [Andrews, 1985].

What is clear is that in many languages, there is one argument role (especially among arguments of verbs), which is the only one to display certain grammatical properties. Which properties these are, however, varies from language to language. Subjects in English have the following properties (among others):

- Control agreement on present tense verbs

- Take nominative case (distinguished in pronouns only)

- Appear to the left of the verb while others arguments appear to the right

- Can be controlled by other arguments in raising/control constructions (see #90 and #91)

However, these properties do not apply universally: In many languages verbs agree with two arguments, rather than just one, or with no arguments at all. Siewierska [2011c] surveys person agreement in 378 languages of which 193 have verbs agreeing with (at least) two arguments and

---

[9]All examples are from Ruppenhofer *et al.* 2010, 65–71.

92 have verbs agreeing with no arguments. Concerning case, many languages don't have case at all (100 of Iggesen's [2011b] sample of 261 languages). Among those that do, some allow at least some verbs to idiosyncratically assign particular cases to their subjects (so-called 'quirky case', see Zaenen *et al.* 1985). Languages with verb-final, verb-initial or free word order (see #78) won't have a distinguished position to one side of the verb for one argument. Finally, it is not clear that all languages have the phenomena of raising and control [Noonan, 2007].

Despite the difficulty of finding properties which uniquely pick out the notion of subject cross-linguistically, it is nonetheless the case that in many of the world's languages one argument of verbs does get special treatment. Even if that treatment varies across languages, we can call that argument role (or grammatical function) 'subject'. In typological work [e.g., Dryer 2011d] it is common to focus on something akin to Dowty's [1991] proto-roles, and speak of the more agent-like and the more patient-like arguments of transitive verbs, though which of these gets treated as a distinguished argument in the sense described here can vary across languages.

#71 Arguments can generally be arranged in order of obliqueness.

Although the properties that pick out specific argument types vary from language to language, Andrews [1985] argues that most languages distinguish *core* arguments from *obliques*. Core arguments include the two arguments of what Andrews calls 'primary transitive verbs' and any other arguments that the grammar of the language treats similarly. Primary transitive verbs are two-argument verbs where one argument has most or all Proto-Agent properties and the other most or all Proto-Patient properties (see #68). Core arguments always include the sole argument of intransitives and both arguments of primary transitives. Depending on the language, they can also include both arguments of other kinds of transitives as well as additional indirect or secondary objects. These cases are illustrated for English in (94):

(94)   a.   Kim slept.

b.   Kim ate the apple.

c.   Kim saw the apple.

d.   Kim gave Sandy the apple.

(94a,b) illustrate the intransitive and primary transitive verb cases. (94c) gives an example where the semantics of the roles associated with the two arguments are not very typical of Proto-Agent and Proto-Patient, but the grammar of English treats these arguments the same as the two arguments in (94b). Finally, (94d) gives an example of a ditransitive verb with two objects.

According to Andrews [1985], it is a hallmark of core arguments that the same syntactic roles (here subject, object, indirect object) can house arguments with very different semantic roles, depending on the verb. This contrasts with oblique arguments, which tend to have a much tighter correlation between the syntactic realization (in English, choice of preposition) and the semantic role.

Beyond the relatively coarse-grained core/oblique distinction, some authors have attempted to create more complete orders of argument types. For example, Keenan and Comrie [1977] propose an accessibility hierarchy which encodes a hypothesis about relative clause formation cross-linguistically: if a language has relative clauses where the head noun corresponds to an given argument within the relative clause, it can also form relative clauses where the head noun corresponds to other arguments within the relative clause that are more 'accessible', according to the hierarchy. Their proposed hierarchy is shown in (95). According to this hierarchy, a language that can form relative clauses where the head noun corresponds to an indirect object of the relative clause can also form relative clauses on direct objects and subjects:

(95)   Subject > Direct Object > Indirect Object > Oblique Argument > Possessor > Object of Comparison

Pollard and Sag [1992] argue that the constraints on possible antecedents of reflexive pronouns (the -*self* forms in English) and non-reflexive pronouns are best stated in terms of a similar ordering of arguments of a given predicate according to obliqueness.

Most discussions of obliqueness seem to concern NP and PP arguments. Andrews [1985], for example, does not discuss clausal arguments. In general, however, oblique arguments are considered to fall between core arguments and adjuncts, so clausal arguments would be less oblique than clausal adjuncts. Clausal arguments are taken up immediately below.

#72 Clauses, finite or non-finite, open or closed, can also be arguments.

While many discussions of arguments focus on NP or PP arguments, it is important to note that in many languages clauses can also be arguments, not only of verbs but also of many different types of heads. (96) shows examples of clausal arguments of verbs (subject and different object or complement positions) in English. The clauses in question are set off in square brackets.

(96)   a. Kim knows [(that) Sandy left.]

      b. Kim knows [whether/if Sandy left.]

      c. [That Sandy left] surprised Kim.

      d. [Whether Sandy left] doesn't matter.

      e. Kim told Pat [that Sandy left].

      f. Kim told Pat [whether/if Sandy left.]

Note that clausal arguments can be declarative (representing statements, as in (96a,c,e) or interrogative (representing questions, as in (96b,f,d)).

Nouns, adjectives and prepositions also take clausal arguments in some languages:[10]

---

[10]Not all linguists would classify *before* as a preposition, but whatever its part of speech, it should not be controversial to say that it takes the clause to its right as an argument and then serves as a modifier of another clause (appearing to the left in (97)).

(97)   a. The fact [that Kim knows] is problematic.

      b. Kim found out before [Sandy told anyone else].

      c. Kim is happy [that Sandy shared the information].

Note that in English, finite clausal arguments sometimes require a complementizer and sometimes do not. The interrogative embedded clauses are all marked with *if* or *whether*, unless they are so-called *wh*-questions, as in (98):

(98)   a. Kim knows [who left].

      b. [Who was in charge] remains unclear.

The declarative clauses require the complementizer *that* in subject position and as the complement of nouns or adjectives. The complementizer *that* is optional for declarative clausal complements as in (96a) and impossible with prepositions (97b).

We also see non-finite clauses serving arguments of various types of heads:

(99)   a. Kim wants [to leave].

      b. [To leave] would be risky.

      c. [For Kim to leave] would be risky.

      d. Kim is happy [to leave].

      e. Kim is happy [for Sandy to leave].

      f. Kim's decision [to leave] didn't surprise anyone.

The clauses in brackets in these examples are non-finite in that they are headed by verbs which are not inflected for tense and thus (according to the constraints on English syntax) cannot serve as stand-alone main clauses. These examples include both open non-finite clauses, where the subject is not expressed within the clause (99a,b,d,f) as well as closed clauses, which do contain their subject (99c,e).[11]

Typological studies suggest that the majority of the world's languages have clausal arguments, at least in complement (non-subject) roles, but not all languages do [Dixon, 2006]. Those that don't use other means to link clauses together and express meanings akin to those expressed by clausal complementation in other languages, sometimes with concomitant increases in ambiguity (*Ibid.*).

#73 Syntactic and semantic arguments aren't the same, though they often stand in regular relations to each other.

The preceding discussion has given an overview of how arguments to predicates can be categorized both semantically (#68) and syntactically (#69–#71). It is important to note that

---

[11]English clausal complements can take still other forms, see Huddleston and Pullum 2002, Ch. 14.

these categorizations represent separate layers of grammatical patterning, and that there is no one-to-one mapping between them. For example, in (100a), the subject plays roughly the same semantic role as the object in (100b), and vice versa:[12]

(100)   a. Kim liked the opera.

      b. The opera pleased Kim.

Similarly, while the most agent-like argument tends to show up as the subject (in active sentences, and in English-like languages), the most agent-like can be quite un-agent-like depending on the sentence.

(101)   a. Kim threw the ball.

      b. Kim saw the game.

      c. Kim sneezed.

      d. Kim died.

Similar remarks can be made about other syntactic argument positions.

In addition, the subject of certain predicates need not play any semantic role with respect to those predicates, as illustrated with expletive subjects in (102) (for more detail, see #89):

(102)   a. It began to snow.

      b. It continues to surprise Kim that Sandy won.

      c. There will begin to be snow flurries this afternoon.

      d. There will continue to be snow flurries throughout the afternoon.

Despite this range of variation, the mapping of semantic to syntactic arguments is not a free-for-all. Each language has a set of *subcategorization frames* which specify the range of syntactic arguments selected by a head, and the linking of those arguments to the semantic arguments.[13] These are discussed further in #75. These subcategorization frames interact with syntactic phenomena which rearrange the mapping of semantic to syntactic arguments, again in systematic ways, such as passive:

(103)   a. Kim wrote this letter.

      b. This letter was written by Kim.

Such syntactic phenomena are taken up in #84–#91.

---

[12]These roles are sometimes referred to in the literature as 'experiencer' (Kim) and 'stimulus' (the opera), but see #68 above on the caveats about such roles as theoretical or descriptive constructs.

[13]However, the exact nature of the semantic relationship between predicate and argument may be entirely lexically specific, see #68.

#74 For many applications, it is not the surface (syntactic) relations, but the deep (semantic) dependencies that matter.

Dependency parsers return structures which make syntactic or semantic dependencies explicit. This contrasts with constituency parsers which return phrase structure trees. The relationship between phrase structure and syntactic dependency structure is more or less direct, depending on the language (see #78), but even when it is relatively direct, an explicit representation of dependency structure can be relevant for NLP applications. A small sample of recent NLP work using dependency information includes: string-to-dependency statistical machine translation [Shen *et al.*, 2010] (inter alios), language modeling [Rastrow *et al.*, 2012], textual entailment [Volokh and Neumann, 2010], and extracting protein-protein interactions from biomedical text [Liu *et al.*, 2010].

For language modeling, syntactic dependencies, being closer to the surface string, may in fact be more important. Where the purpose of the dependencies is to 'get at' the meaning encoded in the natural language strings (as in information extraction, textual entailment, and to a certain extent MT), however, dependency structures which normalize to semantic dependencies are likely to be more relevant. Ivanova *et al.* [2012] contrast the dependency relations captured in a variety of annotation schemes along several dimensions which distinguish more surfacy (syntax-based) from 'deeper' (more semantics-based) representations. Note that because there are words which play important syntactic roles but have negligible or no semantic import (see #88), more semantics-based representations will often not include every word in the input string. This makes them more suitable for meaning-related tasks and less suitable for tasks concerned with well-formed strings.

An example (adapted from Ivanova *et al.* 2012, 7) is shown in Figure 8.1. This example contrasts the CoNLL 2008 syntactic dependency structure [Surdeanu *et al.*, 2008] with a dependency structure derived from the semantic representations output by the ERG [Flickinger 2000, 2011]. Where the CoNLL structure links every word in the structure, the ERG-based analysis does not include *is* or *to*. Note also that the ERG-based analysis makes explicit the semantic dependency between *apply* and *technique*, which is not represented in the CoNLL format.[14]

#75 Lexical items map semantic roles to grammatical functions.

All linguistic theories of grammar include provisions for a lexicon, which is a set of lexical entries. Lexical entries include information that is idiosyncratic to a word (its pronunciation and/or orthography and its semantic predicate), as well as information which might be shared by many other words. This information includes part of speech (#47), other morphological properties (e.g., noun class—see #30), and most relevantly here, information about the syntactic and semantic arguments anticipated by the word and their relationship to each other. These selectional properties together are called the word's *subcategorization frame* or alternatively, its *valence* and

---

[14]This sentence is an example of so-called '*tough*-movement'. For more on this construction and its impact on the ability of parsers to recover semantic dependencies, see #94 and Bender *et al.* 2011.

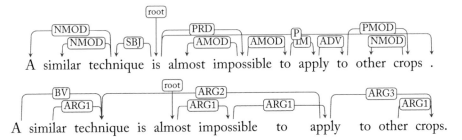

Figure 8.1: Syntactic (CoNLL 2008, top) and semantic (ERG, bottom) dependency structures

the relationship between the syntactic and semantic argument lists is called *linking*. Note that one and the same phonological (or orthographic) form can be associated with different lexical entries, so long as the semantics, POS or other morphosyntactic properties or valence differs between the entries.

The ERG ('1111' release; Flickinger 2000, 2011) distinguishes 193 types of lexical entries for verbs (including types for idiomatic uses and certain frequent types of errors), most of which are differentiated by the range of syntactic arguments they expect.[15] For example, there are two entries for the verb *accept*. One expects an NP subject and an NP complement, as in (104a), but treats the NP complement as optional (see #96). The other expects an NP subject and a clausal complement, as in (104b).

(104)   a. Kim accepted (the challenge).

      b. Kim accepted that it would be difficult.

In the ERG's entries for these words, they both link their subject to their first semantic argument and their complement to the second.

The verb *tell* exemplifies a more complicated set of valence types, including a handful of 'phrasal verbs', as illustrated in (105):

(105)   a. Kim told Sandy a story.

      b. Kim told Sandy whether to jump.

      c. Kim told Sandy to jump.

      d. Kim told (Sandy).

      e. Kim could tell that Sandy left.

      f. Kim could tell by the number of shoes in the hall that Sandy had left.

---

[15]FrameNet, as of March 8, 2013, distinguishes 1162 total frames (`https://framenet.icsi.berkeley.edu/fndrupal/current_status`). This large difference is probably mostly due to the fact that FrameNet represents a wide range of lexical semantic detail which is not represented by the ERG.

    g. Kim could tell whether to jump.

    h. Kim told Sandy about the game.

    i. Kim told Sandy of many things.

    j. Kim told Sandy off.

To pick just one example to look at in more detail, (105f) involves a lexical entry for *tell* which specifies three syntactic arguments: an NP subject, a CP complement and a PP complement which furthermore must contain the P *by*. On the ERG's treatment, the NP subject is linked to the first semantic argument, the NP inside the PP to the second (treating the *by* as semantically empty), and the CP to the third. The predicate contributed by the verb itself is named _tell_v_by, which is differentiated from e.g., the predicate _tell_v_1 introduced by *tell* in each of (105a–e,g).

    Given how much information about dependents (their number and syntactic category) is encoded in the lexical type of a head, enriching part of speech tags with this information and then training taggers to label words with these enriched parts of speech can provide a lot of information about the actual structure of the sentence and narrow the search space for parsers. This is the idea behind 'supertagging' (Bangalore and Joshi 1999, see also Dridan *et al.* 2008 and Dridan and Baldwin 2010 for the application of supertagging to the ERG types described here). Conversely, the range of variation in valence types underscores the importance of lexical resources to grammar-based approaches to parsing, such as those using the ERG.

#76 Syntactic phenomena are sensitive to grammatical functions.

    Grammatical functions (i.e., syntactic roles) are relevant for the description of syntactic phenomena because syntactic phenomena can be shown to be sensitive to them. For example, English present-tense verbs agree with their subjects, regardless of the semantic role of that subject:[16]

(106)   a. The kids throw the ball.

    b. *The kids throws the ball.

    c. The kids see the game.

    d. *The kids sees the game.

    e. The dogs all sneeze.

    f. *The dogs all sneezes.

[16]An exception to this pattern—probably the only one for English—is with the *there* of presentational constructions. This element appears to not have a number value of its own, but rather to take on the number value of the NP after *be* [Huddleston and Pullum, 2002, 242]:

    (i)   There is a book on the shelf.
    (ii)   There are books on the shelf.

    g. It snows.

    h. *It snow.

Many languages have much more elaborate agreement systems than English does, including agreement with non-subject arguments (#79). Other very basic syntactic phenomena which target specific grammatical functions (both subjects and otherwise) include word order (#78) and case marking (#80). More involved examples include raising (#90) or control (#91), where verbs (or other heads, including adjectives) select for subjectless clauses as complements and then link the interpretation of the subject of the embedded clause to another one of their arguments. Again, this is not sensitive to the semantic role of the subject:

(107)   a. The kids continued to throw the ball.

      b. The kids tried to see the game.

      c. The dogs are all expected to sneeze.

      d. It is likely to snow.

#77 Identifying the grammatical function of a constituent can help us understand its semantic role with respect to the head.

Grammatical functions are important to syntactic theory because they help capture generalizations about both basic phenomena such as word order, agreement and case, as well as more intricate (and lower-frequency) phenomena such as relative clause formation, raising and control, and the interpretation of reflexive pronouns (forms like *themselves*). Conversely, these phenomena are useful in NLP (and specifically in parsing) because they provide the outward markers of grammatical function. Information about grammatical functions (i.e., the syntactic roles played by constituents of a sentence) combined with information about the mapping of syntactic to semantic roles provided by each lexical head leads to precise information about semantic roles, which is often the information of interest in NLP (see #74). Even without the detailed lexical information detection of grammatical functions can provide a useful, if noisy, indicator of semantic roles.

#78 Some languages identify grammatical functions primarily through word order.

The world's languages vary in the degree to which they allow for multiple orders of constituents within a sentence (without changing meaning). For example, the two English sentences in (108a,b) do not mean the same thing; those in (108c,d) have a relatively restricted set of contexts in which they can appear in (and may seem ungrammatical out of context);[17] and the sentences in (108e–h) are simply ungrammatical:

[17]Furthermore, (108c,d) don't mean the same thing as each other. (108c) shares its truth conditions with (108a) and (108d) with (108b).

(108)   a. The dog bit the man.

    b. The man bit the dog.

    c. The man, the dog bit.

    d. The dog, the man bit.

    e. *Bit the man the dog.

    f. *Bit the dog the man.

    g. *Man the bit dog the.

    h. *Man bit dog the the.

The first six of these sentences illustrate the major constituent word order property of English, namely that it is an SVO language. In SVO languages, the 'normal' (and usually most frequent) word order in a clause with a transitive verb and two nominal arguments is subject-verb-object. Example (108g) illustrates the fact that the order of determiners and nouns within noun phrases is also fixed in English. Finally, example (108h) illustrates the fact that English generally does not allow discontinuous noun phrases.[18]

In contrast to these properties of English, a language like Russian allows much more flexibility of the major constituents. All of the examples in (109) are grammatical and mean the same thing, though they do have different pragmatic restrictions (i.e., different discourse contexts in which they can be used):

(109)   a. Человек   укусил   собаку.
       Chelovek   ukusi-l   sobak-u.
       man.NOM.SG.M bite-PAST.PFV.SG.M dog-ACC.SG.F
       'The man bit the dog.' [rus]

    b. Chelovek sobaku ukusil.

    c. Ukusil sobaku chelovek.

    d. Ukusil chelovek sobaku.

    e. Sobaku ukusil chelovek.

    f. Sobaku chelovek ukusil.

In certain registers (both literary and colloquial) Russian also allows for discontinuous noun phrases [Sekerina, 1997], as illustrated in (110) (*Ibid.*, 188), where *Interesnuju* 'interesting' and *rabotu* 'work' are interpreted as part of the same noun phrase.

---

[18] An exception this is 'relative clause extraposition', see #95.

(110) Интересную   они   предложили   моей   дочке
       Interesn-uju   oni   predloži-l-i mo-ej   dočk-e
       Interesting-ACC.SG.F 3PL.NOM offer-PST.PFV-PL my-DAT.SG.F daughter-DAT.SG.F
       работу.
       rabot-u.
       work-ACC.SG.F
       'They offered interesting work to my daughter.' [rus]

Several Australian languages are also famous for discontinuous noun phrases. (111) provides and example from Wambaya (from Nordlinger 1998:223).

(111) Ngaragana-nguja ngiy-a   gujinganjanga-ni jiyawu ngabulu.
       grog-PROP.IV.ACC 3.SG.NM.A-PST mother.II.ERG   give   milk.IV.ACC
       '(His) mother gave (him) milk with grog in it.' [wmb]

In (111), the initial word *Ngaragana-nguja* which translates as 'with grog in it' is a modifier of the noun *ngabulu* 'milk' at the other end of the sentence.

Dryer [2011d] surveyed 1,377 languages for their major constituent word order. He found 189 with no dominant order. Among the remainder, the most frequent type is SOV (subject-object-verb; 565 languages, including Hindi and Central Pashto), followed by SVO (488, including English and Mandarin). The remaining four categories are much less frequent: VSO (95, including Modern Standard Arabic and Tagalog), VOS (25, including Malagasy), OVS (11, including Hixkaryana) and OSV (4, Kxoe, Tobati, Wik Ngathana and Nadëb).[19] Among languages with freer orders, there are those that allow any of the six orders of major constituents as well as those that allow variation between just some. For example, some languages are simply 'verb-final', allowing both SOV and OSV.

There is of course much more to word order than the order of verbs, subjects and objects in transitive clauses (e.g., order of determiners and nouns, order of adjectives and nouns, etc.), just as there are many clauses with argument types (grammatical functions) beyond subject and object. Typologists are particularly interested in the major constituent order because it correlates with other properties of languages [see, e.g., Dryer 2007]. For the purposes of NLP the key points here are that (a) relatively fixed word order will mean that position in a sentence is a strong cue for grammatical function, (b) not all languages have this property, and (c) even among those that do, the word order can vary.

#79 Some languages identify grammatical functions through agreement.

One way in which the core arguments (subjects, direct objects, and sometimes even second or indirect objects) get special treatment in languages (as opposed to other grammatical functions)

---

[19]Interestingly, these four OSV languages are all from different language families. Kxoe is a Khoisan language spoken in Angola and Namibia, Tobati is an Austronesian language spoken in Indonesia, Wik Ngathana is an Australian language spoken in Northern Australia, and Nadëb is a Nadahup language from Brazil.

is in agreement phenomena. Specifically, verbs in many languages agree with one or more of their arguments, usually in person, number and/or gender (see #30 and #38–#39). When the arguments of a transitive (or ditransitive) verb have different agreement properties, this information can be sufficient to disambiguate the grammatical functions of the arguments, even in the absence of any other markers.

Siewierska [2011c] surveyed 378 languages regarding agreement in person between verbs and up to two arguments in transitive clauses. In that survey, the most common type was person marking of both arguments (agent-like and patient-like; 193 languages), followed by no agreement in person (82 languages). The remaining categories in this survey were agreement with just the agent-like argument (73),[20] just the patient-like (24), and agreement with either argument (but not both at once; 6).

Siewierska's survey did not consider clauses with more than two arguments, but there are at least some languages which show agreement with three arguments, including Basque. (112) (adapted from Joppen and Wunderlich 1995:129) gives an example of a clause with a ditransitive verb. In Basque (as in many other languages) the agreement markers appear on an auxiliary element:

(112) Zuek   lagun-ei   opari   polit-ak   ema-ten   dizkiezue.
       you.PL.ERG friend-PL.DAT present nice-PL.ABS give-IMPF 3A.have.PLA.3PLD.2PLE

       'You(pl) always give nice presents to your friends.' [eus]

The auxiliary *dizkiezue* is marked for a 3rd person plural absolutive argument, agreeing with *opari* 'present', a 3rd person plural dative argument, agreeing with *lagun-ei* 'friend', and a 2nd person plural ergative argument, agreeing with *Zuek* 'you'.[21]

When linguists look at the function of particular agreement markers across clauses, they find that different languages group arguments differently. Specifically, Siewierska [2011a] looked at agreement marking in transitive and intransitive clauses and discerned the following patterns:

- No agreement marking (84 languages)

- Accusative alignment (212 languages): the sole argument of intransitive verbs is treated the same way as the more agent-like argument of transitives.

- Ergative alignment (19 languages): the sole argument of intransitive verbs is treated the same way as the more patient-like argument of transitives.

- Active alignment (26 languages): the sole argument of intransitives may be treated like the more agent-like or more patient-like argument of transitives, depending on various semantic factors.

[20]English falls into this category.
[21]The arguments here are described in terms of the case marking they bear rather than grammatical function, following Joppen and Wunderlich 1995.

- Hierarchical alignment (11 languages): the agreement properties of the transitive verbs depend on whether the agent-like argument is more highly ranked on some hierarchy (e.g., a person hierarchy 2 > 1 > 3) than the patient-like argument.

- Split alignment (28 languages): Some combination of the above systems.

As with word order, depending on the language, agreement marking can be a useful cue for identifying which noun phrases take which (syntactic) argument position. Unlike word order, accessing the information encoded in agreement markers requires morphological analysis.

#80 Some languages identify grammatical functions through case marking.

Another important morphological cue to grammatical function in many languages is case marking. As discussed in #31, *case* refers to any changes in the form of a noun phrase depending on its role in the sentence. The actual morphological marking may be inflection on the noun, as in the Turkish example in (113), an adposition, as in the Japanese example in (114), or inflection on one or more of the noun's dependents, as in the German example in (115).[22]

(113) Ahmet   Alinin   gazeteyi   Oyaya   büroda   verip   senin   işten
      Ahmet   Ali-nin gazete-yi   Oya-ya   büro-da   ver-ip   sen-in   iş-ten
      Ahmet.NOM Ali-GEN newspaper-ACC Oya-DAT office-LOC give-AND you-GEN work-ABL

      konsere   gideceğini   biliyor.
      konser-e   gid-eceğ-in-i   bil-iyor.
      concert-DAT go-FNomFut-2SG-ACC know-PRS.PROG

      'Ahmet knows that Ali will give the newspaper to Oya in the office and (that) you will go from work to the concert.' [tur] [Kornfilt, 1997, 213]

(114) 太郎　が　　お茶 を　飲んだ。
      Taroo ga   ocha wo non-da.
      Taroo NOM tea   ACC drink-PST.

      'Taroo drank tea.' [jpn]

(115) Das   Mädchen sieht   den   Mann.
      the.N.NOM girl.N.SG see.3SG.PRES the.M.ACC man.M.SG

      'The girl sees the man.' [deu] [Drellishak, 2009, 58]

---

[22]The forms *Mädchen* and *Mann* in (115) are glossed as not carrying any case information. In fact, they carry partial information: If *Mädchen* is used as a singular noun, as it is here, it is compatible with nominative, accusative, or dative case, but not genitive. It could also be a plural form, at which point its case is completely underspecified. Things are a bit simpler with *Mann*, which is unambiguously singular and underspecified between nominative, accusative and dative case. In other German examples in this text, the nouns are glossed with the case value they must carry in context. Here, to illustrate the fact that the case is not directly marked on the nouns, they are glossed as not showing case.

As noted in #31, case can be used only to differentiate arguments or it can be used to mark a range of modifiers. The Turkish example in (113) shows both uses of case: *büro-da* is the locative form of 'office' and this inflected noun is used on its own as an adverbial modifier of the verb *ver-* 'give'. In contrast, *Oya-ya* is the dative form of the name 'Oya', and the dative marking here indicates that the NP is functioning as the recipient argument of the verb 'give'.

As with agreement, the case of the sole argument of intransitive verbs can be aligned to the case of the arguments of transitive verbs in different ways. Comrie 2011 presents the results of a typological survey of case systems analogous to Siewierska's [2011a] survey of agreement systems discussed in #79 above.[23] Among the 190 languages included in the survey, he found the following distribution:

- No case marking (98 languages)

- Nominative-accusative case marking (52 languages): the sole argument of an intransitive is marked like the agent-like argument of a transitive

- Ergative-absolutive case marking (32 languages): the sole argument of an intransitive is marked like the patient-like argument of a transitive

- Tripartite case marking (4 languages): the sole argument of an intransitive has its own kind of marking

- Active-inactive case marking (4 languages): the case marking of the sole argument of an intransitive depends on whether it is agent-like or patient-like.

As noted in #70, within a given language, not all verbs necessarily follow the general pattern of case assignment. For example, the German verb *helfen* 'help' has a use as a simple transitive. While most transitive verbs in German select nominative subjects and accusative objects, *helfen* takes a nominative subject and a dative object, as illustrated in (116), from Drellishak 2009, 58.

(116)   Der   Mann   hilft   dem   Mädchen.
        the.M.NOM man.M.SG.NOM help.3SG.PRES the.N.DAT girl.N.SG.DAT

        'The man helps the girl.' [deu]

Similarly, the Icelandic verb *batnaði* 'recover from' takes a dative subject and a nominative object, while the general pattern in Icelandic is nominative subjects and accusative objects.

(117)   Barninu   batnaði   veikin.
        child.DAT recovered.from disease.NOM

        'The child recovered from the disease.' [isl] [Sag *et al.*, 2003, 126]

---

[23]Comrie looked at full NPs and pronouns separately, as some languages treat these two categories differently with respect to either the presence of case marking (as in English) or its alignment. The results presented here are from the full NP survey.

Even despite this possibility of lexical variation, in languages with case marking, case can be an important cue to grammatical functions. When the case marking is expressed morphologically, either on the noun itself or on one of its dependents, recovering case information once again requires morphological analysis.

#81 Marking of dependencies on heads is more common cross-linguistically than marking on dependents.

Nichols [1986] analyzes morphological indications of grammatical function in terms of where the morphology appears: on the head or on the dependent. Agreement between verbs and their arguments is an example of head marking, where case is an example of dependent marking. Nichols' analysis extends to dependency types beyond the core grammatical functions, including the dependency between the two NPs in possessive constructions, nouns and modifying adjectives, adpositions and their objects, auxiliary verbs and 'main' verbs, and main clauses and subordinate clauses.

In a survey of 60 languages with relatively complex morphology, Nichols [1986] found a strong tendency for languages to be consistent in their marking strategy: languages tend to use either mostly head marking or mostly dependent marking across the syntactic constructions surveyed, and this tendency is even stronger among head-marking languages (because verbal agreement with one or two arguments is common, even in otherwise dependent-marking languages). In addition, Nichols finds that head marking is more common cross-linguistically, both in terms of languages having at least some head marking in terms of the number of languages which are primarily head marking.

Nichols also notes that most grammatical theories are more oriented towards modeling dependent marking, probably because this type is prominent among Indo-European languages. For the purposes of NLP, the main implication here is that models that attempt to make use of morphological information as cues to dependency structure should be flexible enough to handle markers on both heads and dependents, especially when working with resource-poor languages.

#82 Some morphosyntactic phenomena rearrange the lexical mapping.

The preceding discussion has introduced the idea that accurate grammatical description and effective exploitation of grammatical structure in NLP must recognize both semantic arguments and syntactic grammatical functions (see especially #68, #69 and #73). Furthermore, the mapping between syntactic and semantic arguments is mediated by lexical entries (#75) and syntactic grammatical functions can be identified based on morphological and syntactic cues (#76, #78–#80). There is one further piece of information that can be required to accurately map syntactic to semantic arguments, however: Whether or not any mapping-changing syntactic phenomena are involved in the structure of the utterance at hand.

Such phenomena can generally be modeled as (derivational) morphological processes which relate a lexical stem with a certain mapping of syntactic to semantic arguments to another stem with a different mapping, perhaps involving a different number of arguments. In many cases, there is an affix on the derived stem, which serves as a marker of the phenomenon, but this is not always the case. Perhaps the most celebrated such phenomenon is passive, illustrated for English in (118) and Japanese in (119).

(118)   a. The dog chased the cat.

      b. The cat was chased by the dog.

(119)   a. 犬　が　猫　を　追った。
        inu ga   neko wo ot-ta.
        dog NOM cat   ACC chase-PST

        'The dog chased the cat.' [jpn]

      b. 猫　が　犬　に　追われた。
        neko ga   inu ni   o-ware-ta.
        cat   NOM dog DAT chase-PASS-PST

        'The cat was chased by the dog. [jpn]

Passive is discussed further in #84. Other constructions that similarly change the mapping of syntactic to semantic arguments of a lexical item include morphological causatives (illustrated for Japanese and Turkish in (120) and (121); see also #87), reflexive or reciprocal constructions (illustrated for French and Wambaya in (122) and (123)),[24] and benefactives (illustrated for English and Bemba in (124) and (125)).

(120)   a. 鈴木　が　納豆　　　　　を　食べた。
        Suzuki ga   nattou   wo tabe-ta.
        Suzuki NOM fermented.soybeans ACC eat-PST.

        'Suzuki ate natto (fermented soybeans).' [jpn]

      b. 田中　が　鈴木　に　納豆　　　　　を　食べさせた。
        Tanaka ga   Suzuki ni   nattou   wo tabe-sase-ta.
        Tanaka NOM Suzuki DAT fermented.soybeans ACC eat-CAUS-PST.

        'Tanaka made Suzuki eat natto (fermented soybeans).' [jpn]

(121)   a. Hasan koştu.
        Hasan koş-tu.
        Hasan run-PST

        'Hasan ran.' [tur] [Kornfilt, 1997, 331]

---

[24]The reciprocal examples in (122) and (123) involve morphological marking on the auxiliary rather than the main verb. In French this marking involves one of the so-called 'clitics', written with white-space separation, which have been argued to actually be affixes (see #16).

    b. Ben Hasanı   koşturdum.
       Ben Hasan-ı   koş-tur-du-m.
       I   Hasan-ACC run-CAUS-PST-1SG

       'I made Hasan run.' [tur] [Kornfilt, 1997, 331]

(122) a. Les   lions ont   vu   les   oiseaux.
         The.PL lion.PL have.3PL.PRES see.PST.PTCP the.PL bird.PL

         'The lions saw the birds.' [fra]

    b. Les   lions se   sont   vus.
       The.PL lion.PL RECP be.3PL.PRES see.PST.PTCP.M.PL

       'The lions saw each other.' [fra]

(123) a. Ayani ngi   nanga.
         look.for 1.SG.S.(PRES) 2.SG.OBL

         'I am looking for you.' [wmb] [Nordlinger, 1998, 142]

    b. Ayani ngurlu-ngg-a.
       look.for 1.DU.EXC.A-RR-NF

       'We're looking for each other.' [wmb] [Nordlinger, 1998, 142]

(124) a. Kim baked a cake.

    b. Kim baked a cake for Sandy.

    c. Kim baked Sandy a cake.

(125) a. N-ka-lemb-a   kalata.
        1SG-FUT-write-FV c9.letter

        'I will write a letter.' [bem] [Marten, 2011, 183]

    b. N-ka-lemb-el-a   bá-mayó kalata.
       1SG-FUT-write-APPL-FV c2-mother c9.letter

       'I will write my mother a letter.' [bem] [Marten, 2011, 183]

    Note that the English benefactive (124) does not have any particular morphological marking. Two examples (124b,c) are included because the alternation between the NP-PP and the NP-NP frame for this verb on the one hand supports the analysis of the benefactive as an argument of the verb and on the other illustrates the so-called dative alternation, which in itself (independent of the addition of the benefactive argument) is an example of a rearranged argument linking. This will be further discussed in #86. English in fact has a wide variety of such phenomena, which are carefully documented in Levin 1993.

CHAPTER 9

Mismatches between syntactic position and semantic roles

#83 There are a variety of syntactic phenomena which obscure the relationship between syntactic and semantic arguments

The morphosyntax of a word determines its syntactic combinatoric potential. The syntactic structure of a sentence provides the scaffolding on which the grammar of the language builds its (compositional) semantic structure. However, there are many ways in which semantic structure does not directly mirror syntactic structure and especially not simple word sequence. These include phenomena which affect the mapping of syntactic to semantic arguments, discussed briefly in #82. Below, a selection of such phenomena are discussed in more detail, including passive (#84), anti-passives and impersonal passives (#85), dative shift (#86), and morphological causatives (#87). Another kind of mismatch involves semantically empty words, including both function words (#88) and expletives (#89). Raising (#90) and control (#91) phenomena allow semantic arguments of one predicate to be realized as syntactic arguments of another. Complex predicates and coordination add further wrinkles to the mapping from argument constituents to semantic roles: Complex predicates (#92) involve cases where more than one word is involved in the licensing of arguments for a single clause and coordination can produce many-to-one and one-to-many mappings. Other constructions leave the mappings intact, but obscure them in the surface order: Many languages allow syntactic dependents to be realized at some distance from their associated head, either via so-called long-distance dependency constructions (#94) or through 'radical non-configurationality' (#95). Finally, many if not most languages allow some semantic dependents to go unrealized in the syntax (#96–#97).

#84 Passive is a grammatical process which demotes the subject to oblique status, making room for the next most prominent argument to appear as the subject.

Passive is a construction which provides paraphrases by rearranging the mapping of syntactic to semantic arguments. This results in pairs of sentences (called 'active' and 'passive') which have the same truth conditions, but which put a different argument in subject position. Subject position is often given special prominence: For example, subjects are more likely to be topics in English and many other languages [Lambrecht, 1996, Sec. 4.2]. Therefore, while the sentences in (126) are semantically equivalent (true in all the same situations), they are likely to be used in different discourse contexts. For example, (126a) would be a much more natural answer to (127) than (126b).

(126)   a. The dog chased the cat.

      b. The cat was chased by the dog.

(127)   What did the dog do?

     The English passive construction is characterized by a verb which looks morphologically like a past participle. This verb typically combines with the auxiliary *be* (*was* in (126b)), though *be* itself is not present in all passives. Examples of English passives without *be* include *get*-passives like (128a) and passives in non-finite clauses like (128b):

(128)   a. The cat got chased by a dog.

      b. The cat chased by the dog ran up the tree.

An English passive participle maps the semantic argument realized as a subject in active sentences to an optional PP complement with *by*. The next most prominent argument (see #71) is mapped to the subject role. The *by*-PP argument is optional, leading to passive sentences like (129) where the argument corresponding to the subject is not expressed at all:

(129)   a. Precision and recall were measured using the formulas given above.

      b. Mistakes were made.

The core of the passive construction is the passive form of the verb, with its rearranged argument mapping. Though in English passives often involve the auxiliary *be* and the preposition *by*, neither is required, and in fact we see examples without either:[1]

(130)   a. Anyone handed a note will be watched closely.

      b. The horse raced past the barn fell.

     In some other languages, the passive construction involves a similar rearranging of the arguments, but no auxiliary verb. Depending on the language, the 'demoted' argument can occur in a PP or with different case marking. The passive construction in Japanese differs from that of English in both of these ways. In (131b), there is no auxiliary and the 'demoted' subject appears with the dative-marking postposition *ni*,[2] though once again there is characteristic morphology (here, *ware*).

---

[1](130a) is from Sag *et al.* 2003:319. (130b) is the most well-known example of a 'garden path' sentence [Bever, 1970]. Garden path sentences strike speakers as ungrammatical at first encounter, because they are hard to process. This processing difficulty is likely due to competing analyses of the prefix of the string which are so much more probable as to cause the processor to abandon the only structure which can accommodate the full string. In the case of (130b) one relevant source of bias the relative frequency of the intransitive verb *race* and its transitive counterpart, which appears in passive form in this sentence [MacDonald, 1994].

[2]As opposed to the corresponding argument of the active sentence, which appears with the nominative postposition *ga*.

(131) a. 犬　が　猫　を　追った。

inu ga　neko wo　ot-ta.

dog NOM cat　ACC chase-PST

'The dog chased the cat.' [jpn]

b. 猫　が　犬　に　追われた。

neko ga　inu ni　o-ware-ta.

cat　NOM dog DAT chase-PASS-PST

'The cat was chased by the dog.' [jpn]

Passive is reasonably wide-spread in the world's languages: Siewierska [2011b] surveyed 373 languages and found that 162 of them (44%) have a passive construction.

#85 Related constructions include anti-passives, impersonal passives, and middles.

As with many linguistic phenomena, passive represents a category with core or prototypical instances (discussed above) and a penumbra of similar phenomena which nonetheless don't quite have all the properties of a passive. Other phenomena which rearrange and/or suppress syntactic arguments much like the passive include anti-passives, impersonal passives, and middles.

In an anti-passive construction, the patient-like argument is 'demoted' and the agent-like argument takes over the syntactic properties associated with the patient-like argument in the related sentence [Polinsky, 2011, Silverstein, 1972]. The Chukchi (Chukotko-Kamchatkan, Russia) example in (132) from Kozinsky *et al.* 1988, 652 illustrates this phenomenon:

(132) a. ʔaaçek-a　kimitʔ-ən ne-nlʔetet-ən

youth-ERG load-ABS　3PL.SBJ-carry-AOR.3SG.OBJ

'The young men carried away the/a load.' [ckt]

b. ʔaaçek-ət ine-nlʔetet-gʔe-t　　　　　kimitʔ-e

youth-ABS ANTIP-carry-AOR.3SG.SUBJ-PL load-INSTR

'The young men carried away the/a load.' [ckt]

In impersonal passives, the subject is demoted, but nothing is promoted in its place. (In some languages, an expletive subject is required, such as German *es* in (133); see #89.) This construction is not available in English, but it is attested in other languages including German (133) and Turkish (134).

(133) a. Es　　　wurde　　getanzt.

3SG.N.NOM be.3SG.PST dance.PTCP

'There was dancing.' [deu] [Osvaldo, 1986, 595]

b. Es   wurde   bis spät in die Nacht getrunken.
   3SG.N.NOM be.3SG.PST till late in the night drink.PTCP

   'Drinking went on till late at night.' [deu] [Osvaldo, 1986, 595]

(134) a. Burada Pazar   günleri   bile çalışılır.
          Burada Pazar   gün-ler-i   bile çalış-ıl-ır.
          here   Sunday day-PL-POSS even work-PASS-AOR.3

          'It is worked here even on Sundays.' [tur] [Nakiboglu-Demiralp, 2001, 131]

       b. Bütün gece şarkı söylendi.
          Bütün gece şarkı söyle-n-di.
          all   night song sing-PASS-PST.3

          'It was sung all night.' [tur] [Nakiboglu-Demiralp, 2001, 131]

In the middle construction, an argument is promoted, and the erstwhile subject cannot be expressed:[3]

(135) a. This truck loads easily.

       b. *This truck loads easily by movers.

       c. Children scare easily.

       d. *Children scare easily by ghost stories.

With all of these constructions, as with the passive, there are lexical constraints. That is, some verbs can't passivize (136a), don't have middles (136b), etc:[4]

(136) a. *Kim is resembled by Pat. [see Bach 1980]

       b. *This answer knows easily. [Ackema and Schoorlemmer, 1994, 74]

#86 English dative shift also affects the mapping between syntactic and semantic arguments.

Another construction in English which affects the mapping between syntactic and semantic arguments is the so-called *dative shift* alternation [Levin, 1993, 45–49].[5] Dative shift involves verbs which appear with two different syntactic argument frames. Both involve NP subjects, the

---

[3]The examples in (135a,c) are from Ackema and Schoorlemmer 1994:72.
[4]Interestingly, at least some verbs appear to only have passive forms [Bach, 1980]:

   (i)   They are rumored to be CIA agents.
   (ii)   *People rumor them to be CIA agents.

[5]This name is probably due to the fact that languages with richer case systems use dative case for the indirect object of ditransitive verbs. English does not have a dative case.

difference is in the list of complements. In one frame, there are two NP complements; in the other, an NP and a PP (with *to* or *for*,[6] depending on the verb).

(137)   a. Kim gave Sandy the book.

       b. Kim gave the book to Sandy.

(138)   a. Kim sent Sandy the letter.

       b. Kim sent the letter to Sandy.

(139)   a. Kim threw Sandy a party.

       b. Kim threw a party for Sandy.

(140)   a. Kim baked Sandy a cake.

       b. Kim baked a cake for Sandy.

Semantically, the first NP in the NP NP variant corresponds to the PP in the NP PP frame. There is no truth conditional difference between these pairs of sentences, nor are there obvious information structural differences as there is with passive (see #84 above). This word order flexibility does facilitate the ordering of longer constituents after shorter ones:[7]

(141)   a. Kim gave it to the 100th person to buy a ticket after the contest started.

       b. *Kim gave the 100th person to buy a ticket after the contest started it.

       c. Kim gave them the very last tickets available for the last show of the year.

       d. Kim gave the very last tickets available for the last show of the year to them.

   Note that dative shift interacts with passive in interesting ways:[8]

(142)   a. Kim gave the book to Sandy.

       b. Kim gave Sandy the book.

       c. The book was given to Sandy by Kim.

       d. Sandy was given the book by Kim.

       e. %The book was given Sandy by Kim.

Thus in order to work out which syntactic argument is linked to which semantic role in these examples, a parser would need to model both passive and the dative shift alternation.

---

[6]Levin distinguishes the *to* and *for* cases, calling the latter the *benefactive alternation*.

[7](141d) is not nearly as awkward as (141b), probably because *to them* can be stressed.

[8]The mark % on (142e) indicates that judgments for this string vary across dialects. For some speakers, it can mean the same thing as the other examples in (142a–d); for others, it only has the nonsensical reading that Sandy was given to the book.

#87 Morphological causatives add an argument and change the expression of at least one other.

A causative expression is one in which two situations are described: a causing situation in which a causer brings about another situation and the caused situation in which a causee engages in some other action [Comrie, 1989, Song, 2001]. Many languages have a means of expressing such compound situations with one morphologically complex verb. Song [2011] surveys 310 languages and finds that 278 of them have morphological means of expressing causation.

(143) and (144) give examples from Japanese and Turkish, respectively. (143a) and (144a) give non-causative sentences, with transitive and intransitive verbs, respectively. (143b) and (144b) give the causative counterparts. The verbs in (143b) and (144b) each have one more argument than those in (143a) and (144a). In both cases, this argument is the subject. In Japanese, the causee argument appears with dative case in the causative version. In the Turkish example, the causee is marked as accusative. In both languages, there is a morpheme added to the verb (-sase- in Japanese and -tur- in Turkish).

(143) a. 鈴木　が　納豆　　　　　　を　食べた。
Suzuki ga   nattou   wo tabe-ta.
Suzuki NOM fermented.soybeans ACC eat-PST.

'Suzuki ate natto (fermented soybeans).' [jpn]

b. 田中　が　鈴木　に　納豆　　　　　　を　食べさせた。
Tanaka ga   Suzuki ni   nattou   wo tabe-sase-ta.
Tanaka NOM Suzuki DAT fermented.soybeans ACC eat-CAUS-PST.

'Tanaka made Suzuki eat natto (fermented soybeans).' [jpn]

(144) a. Hasan koştu.
Hasan koş-tu.
Hasan run-PST

'Hasan ran.' [tur] [Kornfilt, 1997, 331]

b. Ben Hasanı   koşturdum.
Ben Hasan-ı   koş-tur-du-m.
I   Hasan-ACC run-CAUS-PST-ISG

'I made Hasan run.' [tur] [Kornfilt, 1997, 331]

Note that English does not have a causative morpheme like Turkish and Japanese do, using instead a periphrastic construction with the verb *make*. There are however, classes of verbs which participate in various causative alternations, including causative/inchoative (145), induced action (146), and others (147) [Levin, 1993, 26–32].

(145) a. The door opened.

b. They opened the door.

    c. The vase broke.

    d. They broke the vase.

(146)   a. The army marched through the pass.

    b. The general marched the army through the pass.

(147)   a. The horn honked.

    b. Kim honked the horn.

These alternations are lexically specific in a way that typical morphological causative constructions (like that in Japanese) are not. They only apply to intransitive verbs and only a subset of intransitive verbs at that:

(148)   a. The ghost story scared the children.

    b. *Kim scared the ghost story the children.

    c. *Kim scared the children the ghost story.

    d. Sandy dove into the pool.

    e. *Kim dove Sandy into the pool.

    Morphological causatives can interact with passive, as in the Japanese example (149):

(149) 鈴木　が　田中　に　納豆　　　　　を　食べさせられた。
      Suzuki ga　Tanaka ni　nattou　　　　wo　tabe-sase-rare-ta.
      Suzuki NOM Tanaka DAT fermented.soybeans ACC eat-CAUS-PASS-PST.

    'Suzuki was made to eat natto (fermented soybeans) by Tanaka.' [jpn]

Just as with passive and dative shift, causative constructions affect the mapping of syntactic to semantic roles, most notably in this case the semantic role of the argument filling the subject position. Once again, accurate extraction of who did what to whom requires parsers which are sensitive to the construction. Furthermore, the expression of causative constructions varies across languages, with implications for the design of language-independent NLP systems.

#88 Many (all?) languages have semantically empty words which serve as syntactic glue.

    The previous discussion has looked at syntactic phenomena which rearrange the lexically given mapping of syntactic to semantic arguments (focusing on verbs). Another way in which syntax and semantics can be mismatched is via elements in the syntax which bear no meaning of their own. These are typically grammatical function words which are important to the structure of the sentence but do not contribute any lexical content. They are very common across languages, though languages with more complex morphology probably have fewer independent words which are semantically empty.

Exactly which elements are deemed semantically empty is partially an analytical choice on the part of the grammarian, but is nonetheless constrained by linguistic data. In this case, the relevant data includes paraphrase relations, where alternate phrasings are considered to have exactly the same semantics. Following again the strategy of looking at large computational resources, Table 9.1 lists a selection of the elements treated as semantically empty by the English Resource Grammar (ERG) '1111' release [Flickinger, 2000, 2011].

Table 9.1: Semantically empty elements in the ERG

Type	Examples
Auxiliary *do*	*Did Kim leave?*
Perfective *have*	*Kim has left.*
Auxiliary *will*	*Kim will leave.*
Auxiliary *shall* (in questions)	*Shall we leave?*
Coordination marker *both*	*Both Kim and Sandy left.*
Coordination marker *neither*	*Neither Kim nor Sandy left.*
Copula *be*	*Kim is leaving.*
wh- pronouns in free relatives	*Advise me on who to meet.*
Expletive *there*	*There will be a picnic in the park.*
Expletive *it*	*It surprises Kim that Sandy left.*
Number name *and*	*three hundred and two*
Complementizer *that*	*Kim knows that Sandy left.*
Infinitival *to*	*Kim wants to leave.*
Complementizer *for*	*For Kim to leave would be awkward.*
Complementizer *whether*	*Whether Kim left doesn't matter.*
Complementizer *if*	*Sandy will know if Kim leaves.*
Complementizer *like*	*They look like they want to leave.*
Complementizer *as if / as though*	*They look as if/as though they want to leave.*
Complementizer *but*	*We can't help but notice.*
Selected prepositions	*Kim relies on Sandy.*
including passive *by*	*Kim was helped by Sandy.*

The following are examples of paraphrase pairs motivating the treatment of the underlined words in the examples as semantically empty:

(150) a. <u>There</u> are three bikes on the porch.

      b. Three bikes are on the porch.

(151) a. Kim helped Sandy <u>to</u> pack.

      b. Kim helped Sandy pack.

(152)　a.　Kim gave the book <u>to</u> Sandy.

　　　　b.　Kim gave Sandy the book.

(153)　a.　Kim knows <u>that</u> Sandy left.

　　　　b.　Kim knows Sandy left.

(154)　a.　Kim saw three hundred <u>and</u> two butterflies.

　　　　b.　Kim saw three hundred two butterflies.

　　　Note that in some cases the lexical items analyzed as semantically empty still have semantic impact, just not of a kind best modeled by having them introduce semantic predications. For example, *has* in (155a) contributes information about tense and aspect, but in the ERG [Flickinger 2000, 2011] these are modeled as features on the event introduced by the lexical verb (here, *left*). Similarly, *Did* in (155b) carries tense information and its position in the sentence marks the sentence as a question, but we do not want to say that *Did* means 'past tense question'.[9]

(155)　a.　Kim has left.

　　　　b.　Did Kim leave?

　　　The broader point here is that there are words which do not express a who or a what in the who did what to whom but which are concerned with the grammatical well-formedness of a string and/or the linking of the lexically contentful words to each other. Depending on the task at hand, such semantically empty elements could be very important (e.g., to producing fluent text in generation or to grammar checking) or merely useful (as cues to underlying structure). Syntactic dependency formats (as opposed to more semantic ones, see Ivanova *et al.* 2012) will include such words as both heads and dependents as they typically try to account for every word in the sentence. This can obscure the more semantically interesting dependencies, as the lexically contentful words may be connected only indirectly through some piece of syntactic 'glue'.[10]

#89 Expletives are constituents that can fill syntactic argument positions that don't have any associated semantic role.

　　　One particularly interesting kind of empty element is expletive noun phrases. These are noun phrases which fill syntactic argument positions which are not associated with any semantic role. Not all languages have expletives, and English is unusual in having two: *there* and *it*. *There* is used in existential constructions:

(156)　a.　There are three penguins on the glacier.

　　　　b.　Three penguins are on the glacier.

---

[9]Likewise the complementizers *whether* and *if* indicate that the clauses they introduce are embedded questions, but this is again handled via a feature on events in the ERG.

[10]Figure 8.1 on page 89 provides an example: The relationship between *apply* and *crops* is represented directly in the ERG's semantic dependencies but is mediated by *to* in the CoNLL syntactic dependencies.

The two sentences in (156) are truth-conditionally equivalent: if one is true, the other must be as well. They do differ somewhat in their information structure, as (156a) is specialized for the introduction of new discourse referents in a way that (156b) is not [Lambrecht, 1996, 178]. This difference in meaning must be associated with something in the string, and depending on the analysis that could be the expletive pronoun *there*, the particular variant of the verb *be* or the structure of the sentence as whole. Regardless of which analytical path is chosen, in no case does *there* fill a semantic role with respect to *be* or *on*.

The second expletive in English, *it*, is used in a wider variety of expressions, including weather expressions (157a–c), various idioms (157d–f), extraposition (157g) and cleft constructions (157h) [Huddleston and Pullum, 2002, p. 1481–1483].

(157)   a. It's raining.

   b. It will be foggy tomorrow morning.

   c. It's been dry recently.

   d. They had it out over dinner.

   e. It doesn't pay to gamble.

   f. Kim made it clear that they would leave.

   g. It bothered Sandy that they left.

   h. It's Kim that always leaves.

Expletive *there* is relatively easy to recognize in running text, despite its sharing its orthography with the adverb *there*, because it appears in construction with *be*. The expletive *it* is much more problematic, as the set of predicates it appears with is relatively large, even excluding extraposition and clefts. However, identifying which instances of *it* are expletives can be critical for accurate coreference resolution, as these non-referring items should not be included in any coreference chains. Successfully identifying expletive *it* will most likely rely on detailed lexical resources, such as the lexicon associated with the ERG [Flickinger, 2000, 2011].[11]

#90 Raising verbs provide a syntactic argument position with no (local) semantic role, and relate it to a syntactic argument position of another predicate.

Expletives are NPs which can fill syntactic positions with no associated semantic role by virtue of being semantically empty. However, they are not the only type of argument which can fill such positions. In particular, semantically contentful NPs can appear in such argument positions in the special case of *raising verbs* [Chomsky, 1965, Rosenbaum, 1967, Sag and Pollard, 1991]. Raising verbs are verbs which take a syntactically unsaturated argument (typically an infinitival

---

[11]Bender *et al.* [2011] note that the list of lexical licensers of expletive *it* implicit in the Penn Treebank [Marcus *et al.*, 1993] differs from that in the ERG. The latter is likely more comprehensive, but still not complete.

VP, in English) as well as an NP-type argument which they do not assign a semantic role to. Instead, they link that 'extra' argument to the missing argument of the embedded VP. The verb *appear* is a canonical example of a raising verb in English. The linking behavior is illustrated in (158a), where Kim is interpreted as the experiencer in the liking relation.

(158)   a.   Kim appears to like sashimi.

     b.   It appears to bother Kim that Sandy left.

     c.   There appears to be a party going on.

     d.   Kim appears to be plagued by nightmares.

     e.   Nightmares appear to plague Kim.

The claim that *appear* assigns no semantic role to its subject is supported by the examples in (158b) and (158c), where the semantically empty expletives are unremarkable in that subject position. It is further supported by the fact that (158d) and (158e) are paraphrases, i.e., always true in the same conditions. If *appear* had a semantic role for its subject, then it should be possible to construct scenarios where (158d) but not (158e) is true (or vice versa), by virtue of having different referents in that role.

     Because raising verbs can form unsaturated VPs which are suitable arguments to other raising verbs, chains of raising verbs can separate an NP arbitrarily far from the verb with respect to which it actually plays a semantic role:

(159)   Kim seems to continue to tend to appear to like sashimi.

     Note that the mismatched argument (syntactic but not semantic) need not be the subject of the raising verb. Examples of so-called 'raising-to-object' verbs (alternatively 'exceptional case marking' verbs) include *expect, believe, estimate* and others. In (160), the NP right after the verb (the direct object) is the mismatched argument.

(160)   a.   Kim expects Sandy to leave.

     b.   Kim believes Sandy to have left.

     c.   Kim estimates Sandy to have left early.

That *Sandy* in these examples is a syntactic argument of the higher verb is supported by the interaction with passive (see #84) shown in (161):

(161)   a.   Sandy is expected to leave.

     b.   Sandy is believed to have left.

     c.   Sandy is estimated to have left early.

     Raising (and control, see #91) constructions are not specific to English, but in fact fairly common in the world's languages [Bickel, 2011]. Some of the properties of the construction vary across languages, however. For example, in some languages, the lower clause does not have any unexpressed arguments, but rather an argument that is obligatorily linked to a higher clause, despite being overt [Bickel, 2011, Stiebels, 2007].

Finally, this section has talked in terms of raising verbs, but raising is not restricted to this part of speech. English also has raising adjectives, for example:

(162)   Sandy is likely to leave.

#91 Control verbs provide a syntactic and semantic argument which is related to a syntactic argument position of another predicate.

There is another class of verbs[12] which is closely related to raising verbs, sometimes called *control verbs* or *(subject) equi verbs*. Like raising verbs, control verbs select for a syntactically unsaturated argument (usually a VP) and link one of their other arguments to that open position in the unsaturated argument. Where raising and control verbs differ, however, is that control verb also has a semantic role for the shared argument. This is illustrated in (163a), where Kim is both the experiencer of the liking situation and the agent of the trying situation:

(163)   a. Kim tried to like sashimi.

      b. *It tried to bother Kim that Sandy left.

      c. *There tried to be a party going on.

      d. Kim tries to be plagued by nightmares.

      e. Nightmares try to plague Kim.

      f. Kim tried to be interviewed by the pollster.

      g. The pollsters tried to interview Kim.

Because control verbs have semantic roles for all of their syntactic arguments, the expletives are not suitable arguments for the control verb (even if the embedded VP is the type that takes an expletive subject), as illustrated in (163b,c). Finally, unlike with raising verbs, the choice of which argument of the embedded VP is in the shared position does affect the truth conditions. Thus the (slightly pragmatically odd, yet still grammatical) pair (163d,e) are not true in the same situations, nor are the more ordinary pair (163f,g).

Note that in both raising and control constructions it is always the subject of the embedded VP that is the shared argument.[13] In order to expose a different argument in that position, the

---

[12]And adjectives:

    (i)   Kim was lucky to have left.

[13]This is the kind of property that can be used to motivate a notion of 'subject' across languages, though it won't always pick out the same subset of arguments [Bickel, 2011].

pairs in (158d,e), (163d,e) and (163f,g) take advantage of the argument re-mapping properties of the passive construction.

On the other hand, in control constructions just as in raising constructions, the shared argument does not need to have the subject grammatical function with respect to the matrix verb. Some examples where the shared argument is in other positions are given in (164), where the shared argument is underlined:

(164)   a. Kim persuaded <u>Sandy</u> to leave. [direct object]

       b. Kim advised <u>Sandy</u> to leave. [direct object]

       c. Kim pleaded with <u>Sandy</u> to leave. [PP complement]

       d. Kim appealed to <u>Sandy</u> to leave. [PP complement]

Both raising and control constructions turn on lexical properties of certain licensing verbs (and adjectives). It follows that correctly identifying these constructions in running text, and thus correctly linking up the shared argument with its semantic role in the embedded predicate, relies on detailed lexical knowledge. The lexicon included in the '1111' release of the ERG [Flickinger, 2000, 2011] includes 45 different types of valence patterns for verbs which involve raising or control. The types are instantiated by a total of 501 verbs.[14]

#92 In complex predicate constructions the arguments of a clause are licensed by multiple predicates working together.

Raising and control constructions involve one kind of sharing of arguments between multiple predicates. A related construction type is complex predicates. In a complex predicate construction, two heads (of which at least one is typically a verb, the other may be a noun, adjective or verb) jointly constrain the syntactic properties and semantic roles of the arguments of a single clause [Butt, 2010]. (In contrast, Butt argues that raising and control constructions are biclausal.)

Complex predicates appear in a variety of guises and the exact tests to distinguish them from biclausal constructions vary from language to language. It is typical, however, for them to involve so-called 'light verbs' or verbs with relatively bleached or non-specific lexical semantics as one of the participating predicates. Languages also vary as to the prevalence of complex predicates both in terms of a proportion of lexical types and in terms of token frequency. Thus Butt [2010] notes that while English has complex predicates such as those in (165) (first noted by Jespersen 1965), it's possible to do fairly successful processing of English text without giving these special handling. This contrasts with Urdu, which has only 700 simplex verbs and makes extensive use of complex predicates, such as the examples in (166) [Butt, 2010, 56].

---

[14]These numbers exclude the auxiliaries, which also involve raising.

(165)   a. *have* a rest, a read, a cry, a think

     b. *take* a sneak, a drive, a walk, a plunge

     c. *give* a sigh, a shout, a shiver, a pull, a ring

(166)   a. نادیا نے کہانی یاد کی

     naadyaa=ne   kahaanii yaad   k-ii

     Nadya.F.SG=ERG story.F.SG memory.F do-PERF.F.SG

     'Nadya remembered the story.' [urd]

     b. نادیا کو کہانی یاد اٸی

     naadyaa=ko   kahaanii yaad   aa-yii

     Nadya.F.SG=DAT story.F.SG memory.F come-PERF.F.SG

     'Nadya remembered the story. (The memory of the story came to Nadya.)' [urd]

While some languages have a variety of light verbs which participate in complex predicates, others make heavy use of one single such verb. This is seen, for example, in Japanese where the verb *suru* combines with so-called verbal nouns to jointly license the arguments of the clause:

(167)   スミスさん が　日本語　を　勉強　する。

     Sumisu-san ga   nihongo wo benkyou su-ru.

     Smith-HON NOM Japanese ACC study   do-NPST

     'Mr. Smith studies Japanese.' [jpn]

While the prototypical examples of complex predicates involve two heads, there are also cases (called serial verb constructions) where the description of what is interpreted as one event can involve many separate verbs, which furthermore share at least some arguments. Thai is a language which is particularly exuberant with such constructions. An example (from Muansuwan 2002, 3) is given in (168).

(168)   ปิติ วิ่ง ตรง   ย้อน   กลับ   เข้า   บ้าน   ไป

     Piti wǐŋ troŋ   jɔ́ɔn   klàb   khâw bâan paj

     Piti run go.straight reverse return enter house go

     'Piti ran straight back in the house, away from the speaker.' [tha]

Butt [2010] suggests that serial verb constructions should be distinguished from (core) complex predicates, while acknowledging that the boundary between the construction types can be hard to draw. From the perspective of NLP, both present cases where the relationship between arguments and predicates is made more subtle due to the expression of the predicate, and NLP systems meant to be cross-linguistically applicable should be prepared to handle predicates expressed across multiple words, while allowing for both the combinatorics of such systems as well as lexical idiosyncrasy in possible combinations of the components of complex predicates and their meanings.

#93 Coordinated structures can lead to one-to-many and many-to-one dependency relations.

Many of the world's languages allow for the coordination of arguments and/or the coordination of predicates. Coordination of predicates leads to cases where one constituent serves as a semantic argument of more than one predicate. An example is in (169), where Kim is both the singer and the dancer:

(169)   Kim sang and danced.

Coordination of arguments leads to multiple constituents that in some sense fill one semantic role with respect to the head. In (170), for example, both Kim and Sandy did the leaving.

(170)   Kim and Sandy left.

However, there is an asymmetry in the typical treatment of these constructions. In the analysis of the ERG [Flickinger, 2000, 2011], for example, (169) is taken to involve semantic dependencies between both *sang* and *Kim* and *danced* and *Kim*, while there is only one dependency involving *left* in (170). This dependency is between *left* and the coordinated entity *Kim and Sandy*. Like simplex plural noun phrases, coordinated noun phrases give rise to distributive and collective readings, depending on the predicate [Lasersohn, 1989]. These readings are illustrated in (171):

(171)   a. Kim and Sandy got married in a beautiful ceremony on Saturday. [collective]

      b. Kim and Sandy got married on the same day but 10 years apart. [distributive]

Note also that in some coordinated nominals, the nouns do not refer to two separate entities but rather to two descriptions of the same entity:

(172)   My friend and colleague has arrived.

Depending on the application at hand, it may or may not be important to disambiguate these different readings of coordination constructions.

Languages vary in the ways in which they mark coordination. Regarding the coordination of nominal arguments, the first point of variation is whether the coordination is symmetric (as in English), where the coordinated phrase as a whole fills a grammatical function, or asymmetric, where one coordinand actually fills the grammatical role and the others are modifiers (so-called 'with' coordination) [Stassen, 2000].[15] Among symmetric coordination, there is variation in how the coordination is marked (with an affix, with a separate word, or with simple juxtaposition) and on which conjuncts (just one, all but one, all) [Drellishak, 2004]. Finally, some languages (like English) use the same conjunction to coordinate different constituent types, while others have different markers or even different strategies, depending on the type of constituent (*Ibid*). For

---

[15]Some languages use both types of coordination strategies.

example, while English uses *and* to coordinate any constituent type, the Niger-Congo language Ewe (spoken in Ghana) uses *kple* to coordinate NPs and *eye* to coordinate sentences [Dzameshie, 1998, 72, 73]:

(173)   a.   míe kpɔ Adzo kple Afi
             we see Adzo and Afi

             'We saw Adzo and Afi.' [ewe]

        b.   Kɔku vu   vɔ-a   eye Kɔmi ge   de xɔ-a   me
             Kɔku open door-the and Kɔmi drop PREP room-the in

             'Kɔku opened the door and Kɔmi entered.' [ewe]

In designing systems which extract syntactic and semantic dependencies, it is important to allow for coordinated structures. Because coordination tends to have complicated interactions with several other linguistic phenomena (including notably case marking and agreement), it is generally wise to include coordination from an early stage of analysis. Similarly, in designing systems which use syntactic or semantic dependencies, it is important to consider how coordination is represented in the dependency structures being used, and how that representation relates to the use the dependencies are being put towards.

#94 Long-distance dependencies separate arguments/adjuncts from their associated heads

Another class of constructions which can obscure the relationship between syntactic and semantic arguments are so-called 'long-distance dependencies'. These constructions provide structures in which arguments or adjuncts belonging to one predicate are realized syntactically separated from the predicate, in many cases in a higher clause. They are called long-distance dependencies because arbitrarily many clauses can intervene. The most commonly cited examples involve *wh-* questions (174), relative clauses (175), and so-called 'topicalization'.[16]

(174)   a.   Kim saw the movie.

        b.   What did Kim see?

        c.   What did Sandy claim everyone hoped Lee would believe Kim saw?

(175)   a.   Kim read the book in the library.

        b.   This is the library in which Kim read the book.

        c.   This is the library in which no one believes anyone could imagine Kim read the book.

(176)   a.   I don't think Kim eats eggs. Kim likes to eat BAGELS.

        b.   I don't think Kim eats eggs. BAGELS, Kim likes to eat.

---

[16]This is a misnomer, at least for the English construction illustrated in (176), as the constituent which appears at the beginning of the sentence actually is commonly in the role focus at the level of information structure [Prince, 1981].

c. I don't think Kim eats eggs. BAGELS, I seem to recall Sandy saying Pat had mentioned Kim likes to eat.

In each of the sets above, the (a) example gives a simple sentence without a long-distance dependency to help establish the dependency relations in the other examples. The (b) examples provide a simple case for each construction, and the (c) examples illustrate the ability of these dependencies to stretch across clause boundaries. It's the (c) examples which motivate the term 'long-distance', as they illustrate the fact that the dependency between the head (in the embedded clause) and dependent (in a higher clause) can span multiple clauses. (174) is a straight-forward example of a *wh-* or 'content' question. The dependent involved in the long-distance dependencies in (174b,c) is *what*, corresponding to *the movie* in (174a). *What* is syntactically the object of *see* and semantically fills the role of the thing seen.[17] It's possible to have more than one *wh-* word in a sentence at a time. In English, only one of these appears in the initial position and participates in a long-distance dependency, but other languages including Bulgarian allow the *wh-* words to all stack up at the beginning:[18]

(177)   Who did Kim think read which book?

(178)   Кой   къде мислиш,   че е   отишъл?
        Koj   kŭde misli-š,   če e   otišŭl?
        who.NOM.M.SG where think-2SG.PRES that be.PRES.3SG go.PST.PTCP.M.SG

'Who do you think went where?' [bul] [Rudin, 1988, 450]

(175) illustrates relative clauses with the further twist that the dependent involved in the long-distance dependency is an adjunct (modifier) rather than an argument. As an adjunct, it could potentially be interpreted as belonging to any of the clauses in the long chain in (175c), though the most sensible reading, given world knowledge, is the one in which it belongs to the lowest clause (headed by *read*). Yet another interesting aspect of this example is that the preposition *in* is brought along with the *wh-* word *which*. This phenomenon is called 'pied-piping' [Ross, 1967].

Finally, (176) illustrates so-called topicalization. These examples are given with a preceding sentence for context because the construction is one that places fairly strong constraints on the discourse contexts in which the sentences sound natural. In particular, the sentence-initial constituent has to be interpreted as the focus (also represented with small caps in the example). Such sentences, though actually perfectly ordinary in the right context, often strike English speakers as ungrammatical when presented in isolation.

---

[17]The highest clause in (174b,c) also involves subject-auxiliary inversion and the support verb *did*, as neither *saw* nor *claimed* can appear in an inverted construction in modern English. In (174b) the clause semantically headed by *saw* is the highest clause. In (174c) it's the clause semantically headed by *claimed*. English interrogative constructions involve a wide range of fine syntactic detail like this. For a thorough account, see Ginzburg and Sag 2000.
[18]The fact that the verb *mislíš* 'think' intervenes between the *wh-* words and the clause they belong to (with *ostišŭl* 'gone') shows that the dependencies are long-distance in Bulgarian as well.

These three kinds of long-distance dependencies are not lexically specific. That is, they do not depend on any properties of the predicates involved. So-called 'tough-movement' in English provides an example of a long-distance dependency triggered by a particular set of lexical items. In the examples in (179), the subject of the adjective is interpreted as a semantic (and syntactic) argument of a predicate down inside the infinitival VP or S serving as a complement of the adjective. The ability to mediate the long-distance dependency is a lexical property of the adjectives involved (here, *tough, easy, available* and *dangerous*).

(179)   a. This sonata is tough to play.

   b. This dish is easy to imagine Kim likes to eat.

   c. These tickets are available for anyone to purchase.

   d. This hike is dangerous for inexperienced hikers to take.

Long-distance dependencies are much celebrated in theoretical syntax, and many papers have been written on intricate details of the constraints on these constructions and their cross-linguistic variation. Though much of that fine detail might not be directly relevant to work in NLP, the constructions themselves are important: they can obscure the who did what to whom from simplistic approaches to parsing and they are frequent enough that this could be problematic. Rimell *et al.* [2009] estimate that over 10% of all sentences in the Penn Treebank (combining both the Brown and WSJ sections) include a long-distance dependency of the types they analyzed.

#95 Some languages allow adnominal adjuncts to be separated from their head nouns.

The previous discussion of long-distance dependencies concerned dependents of clause-heading predicates appearing at some remove from their heads. There are also constructions which allow dependents of (non-predicate) nouns to be separated from their heads. The most extreme example of this comes from languages like Wambaya which allow for discontinuous noun phrases. (180) provides two examples (from Nordlinger 1998, p. 133 and 223, respectively):

(180)   a. Babaga-yi   nyi-n   jundurra   mirnda   bajbaga   yardi.
        sister.II-LOC 2.SG.A.PRES-PROG dust.IV.ACC 1.DU.INC.OBL big.IV.ACC put

        'Sister you're making lots of dust for us.' [wmb]

   b. Ngaragana-nguja ngiy-a   gujinganjanga-ni jiyawu ngabulu.
      grog-PROP.IV.ACC 3.SG.NM.A-PST mother.II.ERG   give   milk.IV.ACC

      '(His) mother gave (him) milk with grog in it.' [wmb]

In (180a), *bajbaga* 'big' is a modifier of *jundurra* 'dust', though *mirnda* 'for us', which is not part of the same constituent, intervenes. Similarly, in (180b) *Ngaragana-nguja* 'having grog' modifies *ngabulu* 'milk', though they are on opposite ends of the sentence. The position of *Ngaragana-nguja* in (180b) suggests that this might be the same kind of long-distance dependency as in (176) in #94 above, but the position of the pieces of the NP in (180a) is not consistent with such an analysis. Note that the extensive agreement (in case and gender) between the modifiers and the heads serves to link these elements together, even though they are not contiguous in the string (see #40).

While English and other more familiar languages don't allow nearly as much freedom of word order as Wambaya, there are nonetheless examples of discontinuous noun phrases to be found, thanks to a construction called 'relative clause extraposition', illustrated here for English and German:

(181)   A student walked in [who was wearing pink earmuffs].

(182)   Man   hatte   den   Boten   beschimpft, [der
        one.NOM have.3SG.PST the.SG.M.ACC messenger.SG.M.ACC insult.PTCP, who.SG.NOM
        den   Befehl   überbrachte].
        the.SG.M.ACC command.SG.M.ACC deliver.PST.3SG

        'The messenger was insulted who delivered the command.' [deu] [Kiss, 2005, 285]

#96 Many (all?) languages can drop arguments, but permissible argument drop varies by word class and by language.

#88 and #89 above illustrated cases where syntactic material plays no semantic role. The converse is also possible, namely semantic arguments with no syntactic realization. As discussed in #75, the array of expected syntactic and semantic arguments, and the mapping between them, is a fundamental lexical property of each argument-taking word. There are many different ways in which semantic arguments can fail to be expressed syntactically. One is passive (#84), which allows the demoted subject to be left unexpressed:

(183)   a. Kim made mistakes.

        b. Mistakes were made.

Another is imperative constructions, in which the subject is always the addressee, and need not be overtly realized:

(184)   a. Fix those mistakes!

        b. Everyone fix those mistakes!

Yet another context is raising and control constructions (see #90–#91), where the subject of the embedded verb is left unrealized locally but is interpreted as linked to the subject of the selecting verb:

(185)   a. Kim appeared to fix the mistakes.

      b. Kim wanted to fix the mistakes.

Finally, arguments can simply be left out:

(186)   a. I ate.

      b. I watched.

      c. I'm waiting.

In English, this kind of argument drop is lexically specific. Note that while *devour* and *await* are closely related semantically to *eat* and *wait*, they don't allow their objects to go missing in the same way [Fillmore, 1986]:

(187)   a. *I devoured.

      b. *I'm awaiting.

In addition, English subject drop (outside of constructions such as imperatives or raising/control) is stylistically quite restricted. The examples in (188) would work fine as diary entries, but would stick out as ungrammatical in other genres (e.g., newspaper text).

(188)   a. Ate pizza.

      b. Donated some money at the office.

Other languages (including Spanish) have far fewer restrictions on subject drop, and still others (including Japanese) freely omit nearly any argument:

(189)   Comí   pizza.
       eat.PST-1SG pizza

       'I ate pizza.' [spa]

(190)   a. 見た。
        Mi-ta.
        See-PST

        '(someone) saw (something).' [jpn]

      b. あげた。
        Age-ta.
        Give-PST

        '(someone) gave (something) (to someone).' [jpn]

#97 The referent of a dropped argument can be definite or indefinite, depending on the lexical item or construction licensing the argument drop.

When arguments are omitted via imperative or raising/control constructions, their interpretations are constrained syntactically. When they are omitted via ordinary argument drop, their interpretation is dependent on the verb [Fillmore, 1986]. Some verbs only drop arguments when the referent of that argument can be recovered from context. This is so-called 'definite null instantiation' and is illustrated in (191), where the speaker assumes that the addressee knows what the message was that was told.

(191)   I already told them.

In other cases, the verb encodes expectations about the type of entity filling the unexpressed argument position, but does not require that the actual referent be recoverable from the discourse context. This is termed 'indefinite null instantiation', and is illustrated in (192):

(192)   a.   Kim ate. (a meal)

      b.   Kim doesn't smoke or drink. (tobacco, alcohol)

      c.   They really enjoy baking. (flour-based foods)

The FrameNet [Baker *et al.*, 1998] annotation guidelines [Johnson and Fillmore, 2000, Ruppenhofer *et al.*, 2010] include provisions for annotating dropped arguments and marking whether they are interpreted as definite or indefinite null instantiation.

In languages with freer argument drop, such as Japanese or Spanish, argument drop takes on some of the role that pronouns play in a language like English. Thus (193) is acceptable in a context in which all three arguments are already in the common ground, and can be used in similar contexts to those in which an English speaker would use (194):

(193)   あげた。
       age-ta.
       Give-PST

       '(someone) gave (something) (to someone).' [jpn]

(194)   They gave it to them.

Note that the English pronouns encode a little more information than is available in the Japanese sentence (person, number and gender cues), but this information only goes a small way towards narrowing down the possible referents of the pronouns. The example in (193) should make clear the importance of recognizing dropped arguments, especially those interpreted like pronouns, to MT and other NLP applications: When translating from a language with more dropped arguments to one with less, the system will need to identify the dropped arguments in order to insert pronouns. Even in monolingual applications, however, dropped arguments are important. The more highly topical a referent is, the more salient it is in the common ground and thus the more likely it is to be referred to with a reduced form of a noun phrase — a pronoun, or in many languages, via argument drop [Gundel *et al.*, 1993]. It follows that recovering coreference chains will require detecting unexpressed arguments, as well as those involving overt NPs.

CHAPTER 10

Resources

#98 Morphological analyzers map surface strings (words in standard orthography) to regularized strings of morphemes or morphological features.

The general goal of this book has been to provide NLP researchers with accessible descriptions of morphological and syntactic phenomena and how they vary across languages. Knowledge of these phenomena can inform both feature design and error analysis in machine learning approaches to NLP (see #0). As should be clear from #28–#43, a great deal of information is encoded in the way words are inflected, in morphologically complex languages. For certain applications, simply knowing about this and designing in allowances for lexemes to appear in multiple different inflected forms (with prefixes and/or suffixes) may suffice. If the information encoded in the morphology is important (e.g., for creating factored language models [Bilmes and Kirchhoff, 2003]), however, then the application will benefit from morphological analysis. Similarly, any application involving generation (including machine translation into morphologically complex languages, see Toutanova *et al.* 2008) will benefit from a morphological component that can be run as a realizer.

A well-built morphological analyzer will take surface strings and return underlying forms which isolate the morphemes within words (handling any morphophonological complexity that arises, see #23–#27) while also making explicit the morphosyntactic contribution of each affix. While general methodologies for building morphological analyzers (e.g., finite-state approaches, such as that of Beesley and Karttunen 2003[1]) can be applied across languages, there will always be language-specific work to carry out, either in creating rule sets or in annotating data to support supervised machine learning.[2]

Fortunately, morphological analyzers are the kind of NLP component which can be built once and reused across applications. Examples of robust and widely used morphological analyzers include ChaSen [Matsumoto *et al.*, 1999] for Japanese and the Buckwalter Morphological Analyzer [Buckwalter, 2002, 2004] for Arabic.

---

[1]Finite-state methods have the benefit of being reversible, so that any finite state morphological analyzer can in principle also be used in the realization direction.
[2]While unsupervised approaches to morphological segmentation show some promise [e.g., Snyder and Barzilay, 2008], the mapping to morphosyntactic features is a problem of a much greater complexity for learners with access only to the surface string.

#99 'Deep' syntactic parsers map surface strings (sentences) to semantic structures, including semantic dependencies.

As noted in #1 and #74, for many NLP applications, the most important type of linguistic structure is semantic dependency structure, or who did what to whom. The discussion in #68–#82 motivated two separate levels of grammatical structure (syntactic and semantic) and described the relationship between them and ways in which it can vary cross-linguistically. As with morphology, there are surely NLP tasks and applications for which it will suffice to recognize, in feature design and error analysis, that syntactic and semantic structures are separate but linked and that languages vary in the syntactic means used to identify grammatical functions.

However, when the application at hand requires precise information about semantic dependencies, a parser is called for. Typical treebank-trained stochastic parsers do a reasonable job of recovering syntactic dependencies, especially those closely linked to phrase structure as annotated in the treebank. When it comes to the finer semantic details, especially where syntax and semantics diverge, however, the performance falls off [Rimell *et al.* 2009, Bender *et al.* 2011]. This is partially due to the fact that information not closely linked to the structures as annotated is simply not available to treebank-trained parsers. It can be added via conversion rules as in de Marneffe *et al.* 2006, which in the limit need to be sensitive to particular lexical items (see #89–#94).

An alternative approach is the construction of linguistically motivated implemented grammars. Such grammars are built by encoding linguistic knowledge directly as grammar rules (rather than through annotations), and can be paired with parsing (and generation) algorithms as well as parse ranking (and realization ranking) models to process text. This is the approach taken by the DELPH-IN[3] and ParGram [Butt *et al.*, 2002] consortia, working in the grammatical frameworks of HPSG [Pollard and Sag, 1994, Sag *et al.*, 2003] and LFG [Dalrymple, 2001, Kaplan and Bresnan, 1982], respectively. Both of these groups have developed broad coverage grammars for English and grammars of varying degrees of coverage (and complexity) for a range of other languages, emphasizing efficient development through shared resources and efficient deployment through shared representations.[4] The DELPH-IN resources are in addition all available to the community under open source licenses. Precision grammars, though not developed from treebanks, can be used to create treebanks with a much higher level of linguistic detail and consistency than those created through hand annotation [Oepen *et al.*, 2004]. A very large-scale treebank in this style is available for Wikipedia data, via the WikiWoods project [Flickinger *et al.*, 2010] as is a treebank over the *Wall Street Journal* data included in the Penn Treebank [Flickinger *et al.*, 2012].

As with morphological analyzers, while parsing and generation algorithms can be language independent, the work of developing syntactico-semantic grammars requires language-specific effort. The syntactic complexity overviewed in #83–#97 is only the tip of the iceberg: a broad-

---

[3]http://www.delph-in.net/

[4]The DELPH-IN grammar for English is the LinGO English Resource Grammar [ERG; Flickinger 2000, 2011]. Information about the DELPH-IN grammars is available here: `http://moin.delph-in.net/GrammarCatalogue`

coverage, precision grammar for a language is a very large project, requiring years if not decades of effort developing analyses of a very broad range of linguistic phenomena. Thus for efficient development of NLP technology, it is important to separate grammar development from the development of downstream components which use grammar output, and to reuse grammars for a variety of applications.

In addition, because some linguistic properties are universal (e.g., semantic compositionality or the fact that the meaning of a sentence is built up from the meaning of its parts) and others at least recur across some languages (e.g., SOV word order), it is possible to speed up the development of grammars for new languages by reusing analyses previously developed and implemented. This is the goal of the LinGO Grammar Matrix [Bender *et al.*, 2002, 2010] project, which provides a starter-kit for developing grammars compatible with DELPH-IN technology.

#100 Typological databases summarize properties of languages at a high level.

As important and useful as large-scale hand-built resources can be for NLP, they are available for only a tiny fraction of the world's languages. For some applications, however, even a small amount of linguistic information can be very valuable. For example, Haghighi and Klein [2006] describe a prototype-drive approach to grammar induction. The prototype rules could presumably be developed on the basis of high-level information about a language's word order type. Alternatively, typological information about morphological systems (e.g., prefixing v. suffixing tendencies, #21) could be used to bias unsupervised learners.

Information of precisely this sort is available for a wide variety of languages in the World Atlas of Language Structures (WALS) [Dryer and Haspelmath, 2011].[5] This typological database, cited extensively in this book, encodes information about 2,678 languages across 192 properties. The resulting matrix is sparse (with only about 15% of the cells filled in [Goodman, 2012]), but there are nonetheless 76,492 data points available. As argued in Bender 2011, incorporating such information does not mean that a system is less-language independent. Rather, it allows for the application of machine learning to NLP in ways that are more tuned to the nature and structure of human languages.

Summary

There is of course much more to learn about how language works than can be presented in a short book such as this one. The focus here has been on morphology and syntax, because they are deeply involved in the ways in which languages solve the problem of indicating 'who did what to whom' in string form. Not only is there more to be said about morphology and syntax, there are also other levels of linguistic structure which are highly relevant to speech and text processing, including phonetics and phonology on the one hand and semantics and pragmatics on the other.

[5]http://wals.info

The book has emphasized the ways in which languages vary, with the expectation that such knowledge can be beneficial in the creation of language-independent (or more precisely, cross-linguistically applicable) NLP systems. For linguistics as well as NLP, there are two important lessons from typology: First, languages vary in many ways, and working with only one or a small handful of familiar languages can lead to models and systems which are implicitly tuned to those languages and thus brittle when deployed across a larger sample of languages. Second, the variation is not unbounded, and understanding the range of variation can facilitate the creation of more robust models.

There are not presently other works to recommend which explicitly take the point of view of NLP researchers needing information about language. However, introductory textbooks in linguistics such as *Contemporary Linguistics: An Introduction* [O'Grady *et al.*, 2010] or *Language Files* [Dept. of Linguistics, OSU, 2011] may be of use, as well as the brief chapters in WALS [Dryer and Haspelmath, 2011] which describe each of the properties of language studied there. Beyond textbooks, an excellent way to learn about linguistic structures that are relevant to particular NLP projects is through collaboration with linguists. In general, there is broad scope for collaboration between linguists and NLP practitioners, in model design, feature engineering, and error analysis.

APPENDIX A

Grams used in IGT

This appendix lists all the grams used in the interlinear glossed text (IGT) examples in the book. Each gram is given in the form it appears in in the IGT, followed by a non-abbreviated form, the larger class of grams it belongs to, and pointers to relevant portions of the text.

gram	long form	gram class	see also
1	first person	person	#30, #36, #39, #79
2	second person	person	#30, #36, #39, #79
3	third person	person	#30, #36, #39, #79
A	transitive subject	grammatical function	#69, #70
A	absolutive marked argument	case	#31, #40, #80
ABL	ablative	case	#31, #40, #80
ABS	absolutive	case	#31, #40, #80
ACC	accusative	case	#31, #40, #80
ALL	allative	case	#31, #40, #80
AND	conjunction	coordination	#93
ANTIP	antipassive	valence alternations	#85
AOR	aorist	aspect	#29
APPL	applicative	valence alternations	#82, #83
AtoN	adjective-to-noun	category changing derivation	#12
AtoV	adjective-to-verb	category changing derivation	#12
B	noun class B (specific to Ingush)	noun class (gender)	#1, #30, #36, #39, #40, #41, #79
c[1-9]	noun class [1-9] (specific to Bantu languages)	noun class (gender)	#1, #30, #36, #39, #40, #41, #79
CAUS	causative	valence alternations	#82, #83, #87

D	noun class D (specific to Ingush)	noun class (gender)	#1, #30, #36, #39, #40, #41, #79
D	dative-marked argument	case	#31, #40, #80
DAT	dative	case	#31, #40, #80
DEF	definite	definiteness	#34, #97
DIR.EVD	direct evidential	evidentials	#33
DOBJ	direct object	grammatical function	#69, #71
DS	different subject	switch reference	
DU	dual	number	#30, #36, #39, #41, #79
DUR	durative	aspect	#29
E	ergative marked argument	case	#31, #40, #80
ERG	ergative	case	#31, #40, #80
EXC	exclusive	clusivity (person)	#30, #36, #39, #79
F	feminine	noun class (gender)	#1, #30, #36, #39, #40, #41, #79
FNomFut	future factive nominal	tense, nominalization	#29, #37
FUT	future	tense	#29
FV	final vowel (specific to Bantu languages)		
GEN	genitive	case	#31, #40, #80
HON	honorific		#35
II	class II (specific to Wambaya)	noun class (gender)	#1, #30, #36, #39, #40, #41, #79
IMPF	imperfective	aspect	#29
INC	inclusive	clusivity (person)	#30, #36, #39, #79
INDEF	indefinite	definiteness	#34, #97
INDIR.EVD	indirect evidential	evidentials	#33
INF	infinitive	verb form	#52
INSTR	instrumentive	case	#31, #40, #80
INTR	intransitive	valence	#75
IOBJ	indirect object	grammatical function	#69, #71

IV	class IV (specific to Wambaya)	noun class (gender)	#1, #30, #36, #39, #40, #41, #79
LNK	linking morpheme		
M	masculine	noun class (gender)	#1, #30, #36, #39, #40, #41, #79
N	neuter	noun class (gender)	#1, #30, #36, #39, #40, #41, #79
NEG	negation	polarity	#32
NF	non-future	tense	#29
NM	non-masculine	noun class (gender)	#1, #30, #36, #39, #40, #41, #79
NOM	nominative	case	#31, #40, #80
NPST	non-past	tense	#29
NToV	noun-to-verb	category changing derivation	#12
NUMCL	numeral classifier		#49, #67
O	object	grammatical function	#69, #71
OBJ	object	grammatical function	#69, #71
OBL	oblique	case	#31, #40, #80
PASS	passive	valence alternations	#82, #84, #85
PERF	perfect	tense	#29
PFV	perfective	aspect	#29
PL	plural	number	#30, #36, #39, #41, #79
PREP	preposition		#49, #56
POSS	possessive		#36
PRES	present	tense	#29
PROG	progressive	aspect	#29
PROP	proprietive	case	#31, #40, #80
PSB	possibility	modality	#29
PST	past	tense	#29
POT	potential	modality	#29
PTCP	participle	verb form	#29
REAL	realis	mood	#29
RECP	reciprocal	valence alternations	#82

RR	reflexive/reciprocal	valence alternations	#82
S	intransitive subject	grammatical function	#69, #70
SBJ	subject	grammatical function	#69, #70
SG	singular	number	#30, #36, #39, #41, #79
VToA	verb-to-adjective	category changing derivation	#12
VToAdv	verb-to-adverb	category changing derivation	#12
WP	witnessed past	tense, evidentials	#1, #29, #33

Bibliography

Ackema, P. and Schoorlemmer, M. (1994). The middle construction and the syntax-semantics interface. *Lingua*, **93**, 59–90. DOI: 10.1016/0024-3841(94)90353-0. 104

Agha, A. (1994). Honorification. *Annual Review of Anthropology*, **23**, 277–302. DOI: 10.1146/annurev.an.23.100194.001425. 43

Aksu-Koç, A. A. and Slobin, D. I. (1986). A psychological account of the development and use of evidentials in turkish. In W. Chafe and J. Nichols, editors, *Evidentiality: the Linguistic Coding of Epistemology*, pages 159–167. Ablex, Norwood, New Jersey. 42

Albright, A. (2000). The productivity of infixation in Lakhota. UCLA. Available from `http://web.mit.edu/albright/www/papers/Albright-LakhotaInfixation.pdf`. 12

Alegre, M. and Gordon, P. (1999). Frequency effects and the representational status of regular inflections. *Journal of Memory and Language*, **40**, 41–61. DOI: 10.1006/jmla.1998.2607. 17

Anderson, S. R. (1992). *A-Morphous Morphology*. Cambridge University Press, Cambridge. DOI: 10.1017/CBO9780511586262. 11

Anderson, S. R. (1993). Wackernagel's revenge: Clitics, morphology and the syntax of second position. *Language*, **69**(1), 68–98. DOI: 10.2307/416416. 23

Anderson, S. R. (2006). Morphology. In *Encyclopedia of Cognitive Science*. John Wiley & Sons, Ltd. DOI: 10.1002/0470018860.s00223. 16

Andrews, A. (1985). The major functions of the noun phrase. In T. Shopen, editor, *Language Typology and Syntactic Description, Vol. I: Clause Structure*, pages 62–154. Cambridge University Press, Cambridge. 79, 83, 84, 85

Arad, M. (2005). *Roots and Patterns: Hebrew Morphosyntax*. Springer, Dordrecht. 12

Asahara, M. and Matsumoto, Y. (2000). Extended models and tools for high-performance part-of-speech tagger. In *Proceedings of the 18th International Conference on Computational Linguistics, COLING 2000*, pages 21–27, Saarbrücken, Germany. DOI: 10.3115/990820.990824. 20

Babko-Malaya, O. (2005). PropBank annotation guidelines. Available online: `http://verbs.colorado.edu/~mpalmer/projects/ace/PBguidelines.pdf`. 74

Bach, E. W. (1980). In defense of passive. *Linguistics and Philosophy*, **3**(3), 297–341. DOI: 10.1007/BF00401689. 104

Baker, C. F., Fillmore, C. J., and Lowe, J. B. (1998). The Berkeley FrameNet project. In *Proceedings of the 36th Annual Meeting of the Association for Computational Linguistics and 17th International Conference on Computational Linguistics, Volume 1*, pages 86–90, Montréal, Canada. Association for Computational Linguistics. DOI: 10.3115/980845.980860. 66, 67, 77, 81, 121

Baldwin, T. (2005). Bootstrapping deep lexical resources: Resources for courses. In *Proceedings of the ACL-SIGLEX Workshop on Deep Lexical Acquisition*, pages 67–76, Ann Arbor, Michigan. Association for Computational Linguistics. DOI: 10.3115/1631850. 66

Bangalore, S. and Joshi, A. K. (1999). Supertagging: An approach to almost parsing. *Computational Linguistics*, **25**(2), 237–265. 90

Beesley, K. R. and Karttunen, L. (2003). *Finite State Morphology*. CSLI Publications, Stanford CA. 123

Bender, E. M. (2011). On achieving and evaluating language independence in NLP. *Linguistic Issues in Language Technology*, **6**(3), 1–26. 5, 8, 125

Bender, E. M. and Siegel, M. (2004). Implementing the syntax of Japanese numeral classifiers. In *Proceedings of IJCNLP-04*, pages 398–405. DOI: 10.1007/978-3-540-30211-7_66. 76

Bender, E. M., Flickinger, D., and Oepen, S. (2002). The grammar matrix: An open-source starter-kit for the rapid development of cross-linguistically consistent broad-coverage precision grammars. In J. Carroll, N. Oostdijk, and R. Sutcliffe, editors, *Proceedings of the Workshop on Grammar Engineering and Evaluation at the 19th International Conference on Computational Linguistics*, pages 8–14, Taipei, Taiwan. 125

Bender, E. M., Drellishak, S., Fokkens, A., Poulson, L., and Saleem, S. (2010). Grammar customization. *Research on Language & Computation*, pages 1–50. 10.1007/s11168-010-9070-1. DOI: 10.1007/s11168-010-9070-1. 125

Bender, E. M., Flickinger, D., Oepen, S., and Zhang, Y. (2011). Parser evaluation over local and non-local deep dependencies in a large corpus. In *Proceedings of the 2011 Conference on Empirical Methods in Natural Language Processing*, pages 397–408, Edinburgh, Scotland, UK. Association for Computational Linguistics. 88, 110, 124

Bever, T. (1970). The cognitive basis for linguistic structure. In J. R. Hayes, editor, *Cognition and the Development of Language*. Wiley, New York. 102

Bickel, B. (2011). Grammatical relations typology. In J. J. Song, editor, *The Oxford Handbook of Language Typology*, pages 399–444. Oxford University Press, Oxford. DOI: 10.1093/oxfordhb/9780199281251.001.0001. 111, 112

Bickel, B. and Nichols, J. (2011a). Exponence of selected inflectional formatives. In M. S. Dryer and M. Haspelmath, editors, *The World Atlas of Language Structures Online*. Max Planck Digital Library, Munich. 27, 37, 47

Bickel, B. and Nichols, J. (2011b). Fusion of selected inflectional formatives. In M. S. Dryer and M. Haspelmath, editors, *The World Atlas of Language Structures Online*. Max Planck Digital Library, Munich. 27

Bickel, B., Comrie, B., and Haspelmath, M. (2008). The Leipzig glossing rules: Conventions for interlinear morpheme-by-morpheme glosses. Max Planck Institute for Evolutionary Anthropology and Department of Linguistics, University of Leipzig. 2

Bies, A., Ferguson, M., Katz, K., and MacIntyre, R. (1995). Bracketing guidelines for treebank II style Penn Treebank project. Available from http://www.ldc.upenn.edu/Catalog/docs/LDC99T42/prsguid1.pdf. 80, 81

Bilmes, J. A. and Kirchhoff, K. (2003). Factored language models and generalized parallel backoff. In *Proceedings of HLT/NACCL, 2003*, pages 4–6. DOI: 10.3115/1073483.1073485. 58, 123

Blake, B. J. (2001). *Case*. Cambridge University Press, Cambridge, second edition. DOI: 10.1017/CBO9781139164894. 40

Blake, F. R. (1930). A semantic analysis of case. In J. T. Hatfield, W. Leopold, and A. J. F. Zieglschmid, editors, *Curme Volume of Linguistic Studies (Language Monographs 7)*, pages 34–49. Linguistic Society of America, Baltimore MD. 80

Booij, G. (1990). The boundary between morhpology and syntax: Separable complex verbs in Dutch. *Yearbook of Morphology*, **3**, 45–63. 76

Brentari, D. (1998). *A Prosodic Model of Sign Language Phonology*. The MIT Press, Cambridge, MA. 13

Bresnan, J. (2001). *Lexical-Functional Syntax*. Blackwell, Oxford. 81

Bresnan, J. and Mchombo, S. A. (1987). Topic, pronoun, and agreement in Chicheŵa. *Language*, **63**(4), 741–782. DOI: 10.2307/415717. 50

Brinton, L. J. and Traugott, E. C. (2005). *Lexicalization and Language Change*. Cambridge University Press, Cambridge. DOI: 10.1017/CBO9780511615962. 16, 17

Browne, W. (1974). On the problem of enclitic placement in Serbo-Croatian. In R. D. Brecht and C. V. Chvany, editors, *Slavic Transformational Syntax*, volume 10, pages 36–52. University of Michigan, Ann Arbor. 23

Buckwalter, T. (2002). Buckwalter Arabic morphological analyzer version 1.0. Linguistic Data Consortium; Catalog number LDC2002L49 and ISBN 1-58563-257-0. 123

Buckwalter, T. (2004). Issues in Arabic orthography and morphology analysis. In A. Farghaly and K. Megerdoomian, editors, *COLING 2004 Computational Approaches to Arabic Script-based Languages*, pages 31–34, Geneva, Switzerland. COLING. 123

Butt, M. (2010). The light verb jungle: Still hacking away. In M. Amberber, B. Baker, and M. Harvey, editors, *Complex Predicates: Cross-Linguistic Perspectives on Event Structure*, pages 48–78. Cambridge University Press, Cambridge. DOI: 10.1017/CBO9780511712234. 113, 114

Butt, M., Dyvik, H., King, T. H., Masuichi, H., and Rohrer, C. (2002). The parallel grammar project. In J. Carroll, N. Oostdijk, and R. Sutcliffe, editors, *Proceedings of the Workshop on Grammar Engineering and Evaluation at the 19th International Conference on Computational Linguistics*, pages 1–7. 124

Bybee, J. L. (1985). *Morphology: A Study of the Relation between Meaning and Form*. John Benjamins, Amsterdam and Philadelphia. 33

Chomsky, N. (1965). *Aspects of the Theory of Syntax*. MIT Press, Cambridge, MA. 110

Chomsky, N. (1970). Remarks on nominalization. In R. A. Jacobs and P. S. Rosenbaum, editors, *Readings in English Transformational Grammar*, pages 184–221. Ginn, Waltham MA. 67

Chomsky, N. (1981). *Lectures on Government and Binding*. Foris, Dordrecht. 79

Clark, H. H. (1996). *Using Language*. Cambridge University Press, Cambridge. DOI: 10.1017/CBO9780511620539. 54

Comrie, B. (1985). *Tense*. Cambridge University Press, Cambridge. DOI: 10.1017/CBO9781139165815. 36

Comrie, B. (1989). *Language Universals & Linguistic Typology*. Basil Blackwell Publishing Limited, Oxford, second edition. 6, 106

Comrie, B. (2011). Alignment of case marking of full noun phrases. In M. S. Dryer and M. Haspelmath, editors, *The World Atlas of Language Structures Online*. Max Planck Digital Library, Munich. 96

Corbett, G. G. (1991). *Gender*. Cambridge University Press, Cambridge. DOI: 10.1017/CBO9781139166119. 39

Corbett, G. G. (2000). *Number*. Cambridge University Press, Cambridge. DOI: 10.1017/CBO9781139164344. 38, 51

Corbett, G. G. (2006). *Agreement*. Cambridge University Press, Cambridge. 47

Councill, I., McDonald, R., and Velikovich, L. (2010). What's great and what's not: Learning to classify the scope of negation for improved sentiment analysis. In *Proceedings of the Workshop on Negation and Speculation in Natural Language Processing*, pages 51–59, Uppsala, Sweden. University of Antwerp. 42

Cysouw, M. (2003). *The Paradigmatic Structure of Person Marking*. Oxford University Press, Oxford. 38

Dahl, Ö. and Velupillai, V. (2011a). The future tense. In M. S. Dryer and M. Haspelmath, editors, *The World Atlas of Language Structures Online*. Max Planck Digital Library, Munich. 36

Dahl, Ö. and Velupillai, V. (2011b). The past tense. In M. S. Dryer and M. Haspelmath, editors, *The World Atlas of Language Structures Online*. Max Planck Digital Library, Munich. 36, 51

Dahl, Ö. and Velupillai, V. (2011c). Perfective/imperfective aspect. In M. S. Dryer and M. Haspelmath, editors, *The World Atlas of Language Structures Online*. Max Planck Digital Library, Munich. 36

Dalrymple, M. (2001). *Lexical Functional Grammar*. Academic Press, San Diego. 124

Daumé III, H. (2009). Non-parametric Bayesian areal linguistics. In *Proceedings of Human Language Technologies: The 2009 Annual Conference of the North American Chapter of the Association for Computational Linguistics*, pages 593–601, Boulder, Colorado. Association for Computational Linguistics. 6

Daumé III, H. and Campbell, L. (2007). A Bayesian model for discovering typological implications. In *Proceedings of the 45th Annual Meeting of the Association of Computational Linguistics*, pages 65–72, Prague, Czech Republic. Association for Computational Linguistics. 6

de Haan, F. (2011a). Coding of evidentiality. In M. S. Dryer and M. Haspelmath, editors, *The World Atlas of Language Structures Online*. Max Planck Digital Library, Munich. 42

de Haan, F. (2011b). Semantic distinctions of evidentiality. In M. S. Dryer and M. Haspelmath, editors, *The World Atlas of Language Structures Online*. Max Planck Digital Library, Munich. 42

de Marneffe, M.-C. and Manning, C. D. (2008). The Stanford typed dependencies representation. In *Coling 2008: Proceedings of the Workshop on Cross-Framework and Cross-Domain Parser Evaluation*, pages 1–8, Manchester, UK. Coling 2008 Organizing Committee. 81

de Marneffe, M.-C. and Manning, C. D. (2011). Stanford typed dependencies manual. Revised for Stanford Parser v. 1.6.9. `http://nlp.stanford.edu/software/dependencies_manual.pdf`. 81, 82

de Marneffe, M.-C., MacCartney, B., and Manning, C. D. (2006). Generating typed dependencies from phrase structure trees. In *Proceedings of the Fifth International Conference on Language Resources and Evaluation (LREC'06)*, pages 449–454. 124

Department of Linguistics (2011). *Language Files: Materials for an Introduction to Language and Linguistics*. Ohio State University Press, 11th edition. 126

de Saussure, F. (1916). *Course in General Linguistics*. McGraw Hill. Published in 1959. 65

de Waard, A. (2010). Realm traversal in biological discourse: From model to experiment and back again. In *Proceedings of the Workshop on Multidisciplinary Perspectives on Signalling Text Organisation (MAD 2010)*, Moissac, France. 37

Dixon, R. (1977). Where have all the adjectives gone? *Studies in Language*, **1**, 19–80. DOI: 10.1075/sl.1.1.04dix. 59

Dixon, R. (2004). *Adjective Classes in Typological Perspective*. Oxford University Press, Oxford. 59

Dixon, R. (2006). Complement clauses and complementation strategies in typological perspective. In R. Dixon and A. Y. Aikhenvald, editors, *Complementation: A Cross-Linguistic Typology*, pages 1–48. Oxford University Press, Oxford. 86

Dowty, D. R. (1989). On the semantic content of the notion 'thematic role'. In B. Partee, G. Chierchia, and R. Turner, editors, *Properties, Types and Meanings*, volume II, pages 69–130. Kluwer, Dordrecht. 79

Dowty, D. R. (1991). Thematic proto-roles and argument selection. *Language*, **67**(3), 547–619. DOI: 10.2307/415037. 79, 80, 84

Drellishak, S. (2004). A survey of coordination in the world's languages. MA thesis, University of Washington. 115

Drellishak, S. (2009). *Widespread But Not Universal: Improving the Typological Coverage of the Grammar Matrix*. Ph.D. thesis, University of Washington. 38, 95, 96

Dridan, R. and Baldwin, T. (2010). Unsupervised parse selection for HPSG. In *Proceedings of the 2010 Conference on Empirical Methods in Natural Language Processing*, pages 694–704, Cambridge, MA. Association for Computational Linguistics. 90

Dridan, R., Kordoni, V., and Nicholson, J. (2008). Enhancing performance of lexicalised grammars. In *Proceedings of ACL-08: HLT*, pages 613–621, Columbus, Ohio. Association for Computational Linguistics. 90

Dryer, M. S. (2005). Genealogical language list. In M. Haspelmath, M. S. Dryer, D. Gil, and B. Comrie, editors, *The World Atlas of Language Structures*, pages 584–644. Oxford University Press. 7

Dryer, M. S. (2007). Word order. In T. Shopen, editor, *Language Typology and Syntactic Description, Vol 1: Clause Structure*, pages 61–131. Cambridge University Press, Cambridge, second edition. 93

Dryer, M. S. (2011a). Definite articles. In M. S. Dryer and M. Haspelmath, editors, *The World Atlas of Language Structures Online*. Max Planck Digital Library, Munich. 43

Dryer, M. S. (2011b). Indefinite articles. In M. S. Dryer and M. Haspelmath, editors, *The World Atlas of Language Structures Online*. Max Planck Digital Library, Munich. 43

Dryer, M. S. (2011c). Negative morphemes. In M. S. Dryer and M. Haspelmath, editors, *The World Atlas of Language Structures Online*. Max Planck Digital Library, Munich. 41

Dryer, M. S. (2011d). Order of subject, object and verb. In M. S. Dryer and M. Haspelmath, editors, *The World Atlas of Language Structures Online*. Max Planck Digital Library, Munich. 84, 93

Dryer, M. S. (2011e). Polar questions. In M. S. Dryer and M. Haspelmath, editors, *The World Atlas of Language Structures Online*. Max Planck Digital Library, Munich. 46

Dryer, M. S. (2011f). Prefixing vs. suffixing in inflectional morphology. In M. S. Dryer and M. Haspelmath, editors, *The World Atlas of Language Structures Online*. Max Planck Digital Library, Munich. 25, 26

Dryer, M. S. and Haspelmath, M., editors (2011). *The World Atlas of Language Structures Online*. Max Planck Digital Library, Munich, 2011 edition. 9, 51, 125, 126

Dzameshie, A. K. (1998). Structures of coordination in Ewe. **XXVII**(1), 71–81. 116

Emonds, J. E. (1976). *A Transformational Approach to English Syntax*. Academic Press, New York. 64

Engdahl, E. (1983). Parasitic gaps. *Linguistics and Philosophy*, **6**(1), 5–34. DOI: 10.1007/BF00868088. 4

Epstein, S. and Hornstein, N. (2005). Letter on 'the future of language'. *Language*, **81**, 3–6. 53

Evans, N. (1995). *A Grammar of Kayardild. With Historical-Comparative Notes on Tangkic*, volume 15 of *Mouton Grammar Library*. Mouton de Gruyter, Berlin. DOI: 10.1515/9783110873733. 37

Feldman, H. (1986). *A Grammar of Awtuw*, volume 94 of *Pacific Linguistics, Series B*. Australian National University, Canberra. 69

Fellbaum, C., editor (1998). *WordNet: An Electronic Lexical Database*. Cambridge, MA. 19

Fillmore, C. J. (1968). The case for case. In E. Bach and R. Harms, editors, *Universals in Linguistic Theory*. Holt, Rinehart and Winston, New York. 79

Fillmore, C. J. (1986). Pragmatically controlled zero anaphora. In *Proceedings of the Twelfth Annual Meeting of the Berkeley Linguistics Society*, pages 95–107. 120, 121

Fillmore, C. J. and Baker, C. F. (2004). The evolution of FrameNet annotation practices. In *Workshop on Building Lexical Resources from Semantically Annotated Corpora at LREC'04*, pages 1–8. 65

Flickinger, D. (2000). On building a more efficient grammar by exploiting types. *Natural Language Engineering (Special Issue on Efficient Processing with HPSG)*, **6**(1), 15–28. DOI: 10.1017/S1351324900002370. 19, 61, 70, 73, 77, 80, 88, 89, 108, 109, 110, 113, 115, 124

Flickinger, D. (2011). Accuracy v. robustness in grammar engineering. In E. M. Bender and J. E. Arnold, editors, *Language from a Cognitive Perspective: Grammar, Usage and Processing*, pages 31–50. CSLI Publications, Stanford, CA. 61, 71, 73, 77, 80, 88, 89, 108, 109, 110, 113, 115, 124

Flickinger, D., Lønning, J. T., Dyvik, H., Oepen, S., and Bond, F. (2005). SEM-I rational MT. Enriching deep grammars with a semantic interface for scalable machine translation. In *Proceedings of the 10th Machine Translation Summit*, pages 165–172, Phuket, Thailand. 80

Flickinger, D., Oepen, S., and Ytrestøl, G. (2010). WikiWoods: Syntacto-semantic annotation for English Wikipedia. In N. Calzolari, K. Choukri, B. Maegaard, J. Mariani, J. Odijk, S. Piperidis, M. Rosner, and D. Tapias, editors, *Proceedings of the Seventh conference on International Language Resources and Evaluation (LREC'10)*, Valletta, Malta. European Language Resources Association (ELRA). 124

Flickinger, D., Kordoni, V., and Zhang, Y. (2012). DeepBank: A dynamically annotated treebank of the Wall Street Journal. In *Proceedings of 11th International Workshop on Treebanks and Linguistic Theories*. 124

Francis, W. N. and Kučera, H. (1982). *Frequency Analysis of English Usage. Lexicon and Grammar*. Houghton Mifflin, Boston. 58

Fries, C. C. (1952). *The Structure of English: An Introduction to the Construction of English Sentences.* London : Longman. 58

Gary, J. O. and Gamal-Eldin, S. (1982). *Cairene Egyptian Colloquial Arabic*, volume 6 of *Lingua Descriptive Studies.* North-Holland, Amsterdam. 43

Gazdar, G. and Mellish, C. (1989). *Natural Language Processing in PROLOG: An Introduction to Computational Linguistics.* Addison-Wesley Publishing Company, Reading MA. 29

Georgi, R., Xia, F., and Lewis, W. (2010). Comparing language similarity across genetic and typologically-based groupings. In *Proceedings of the 23rd International Conference on Computational Linguistics (Coling 2010)*, pages 385–393, Beijing, China. Coling 2010 Organizing Committee. 6

Ginzburg, J. and Sag, I. A. (2000). *Interrogative Investigations: The Form, Meaning and Use of English Interrogatives.* CSLI, Stanford, CA. 117

Göksel, A. and Kerslake, C. (2005). *Turkish: A Comprehensive Grammar.* Routledge, London and New York. DOI: 10.4324/9780203340769. 15, 26, 30

Goldberg, A. E. (1995). *Constructions: A Construction Grammar Approach to Argument Structure.* University of Chicago Press, Chicago. 66

Goldsmith, J. and Reutter, T. (1998). Automatic collection and analysis of German compounds. In *Proceedings of the COLING/ACL Workshop on the Computational Treatment of Nominals*, pages 61–69. 15

Good, J. (2011). The typology of templates. *Language and Linguistics Compass*, 5(10), 731–747. DOI: 10.1111/j.1749-818X.2011.00306.x. 21

Goodman, M. W. (2012). Augmenting WALS with inferred feature values. Unpublished ms., University of Washington. 125

Greenberg, J. (1963). Some universals of grammar with particular reference to the order of meaningful elements. In *Univerals of Language*, pages 73–113. MIT Press, Cambridge. 6

Greenberg, J. H. (1960). A quantitative approach to the morphological typology of language. *International Journal of American Linguistics*, 26(3), 178–194. DOI: 10.1086/464575. 24

Gruber, J. S. (1965). *Studies in Lexical Relations.* Ph.D. thesis, MIT. 79

Guevara, E. and Scalise, S. (2009). Searching for universals in compounding. In S. Scalise, E. Magni, and A. Bisetto, editors, *Universals of Language Today*, pages 100–128. Springer. 15

Gundel, J., Hedberg, N., and Zacharski, R. (1993). Cognitive status and the from of referring expressions in discourse. *Language*, 69(2), 274–307. DOI: 10.2307/416535. 43, 122

Haghighi, A. and Klein, D. (2006). Prototype-driven grammar induction. In *Proceedings of the 21st International Conference on Computational Linguistics and 44th Annual Meeting of the Association for Computational Linguistics*, pages 881–888, Sydney, Australia. Association for Computational Linguistics. DOI: 10.3115/1220175.1220286. 125

Hajič, J., Böhmová, A., Hajičová, E., and Hladká, B. (2000). The Prague Dependency Treebank: A three-level annotation scenario. In A. Abeillé, editor, *Treebanks: Building and Using Parsed Corpora*, pages 103–207. Kluwer, Amsterdam. DOI: 10.1007/978-94-010-0201-1_10. 61

Hammarström, H. (2007). *Handbook of Descriptive Language Knowledge: A Full-Scale Reference Guide for Typologists*. Number 22 in LINCOM handbooks in linguistics. LINCOM. 7

Hankamer, J. (1989). Morphological parsing and the lexicon. In W. Marlsen-Wilson, editor, *Lexical Representation and Process*, pages 392–408. The MIT Press, Cambridge MA. 29

Haugereid, P. (2004). Linking in constructions. In S. Müller, editor, *Proceedings of the HPSG-2004 Conference, Center for Computational Linguistics, Katholieke Universiteit Leuven*, pages 414–422. CSLI Publications, Stanford. 66

Hawkins, J. A. (2000). The relative order of prepositional phrases in English: Going beyond manner-place-time. *Language Variation and Change*, **11**, 231–266. 71, 77

Hengeveld, K. (1992). Parts of speech. In M. Fortescue, P. Harder, and L. Kristoffersen, editors, *Layered Structure and Reference in a Functional Perspective*, pages 29–55. Benjamins, Amsterdam. 58

Hinds, J. (1986). *Japanese*. Routledge, New York. 30

Hoijer, H. (1971). Athapaskan morphology. In J. Sawyer, editor, *Studies in American Indian Languages*, pages 113–147. University of California, Berkeley. 21

Hopper, P. J. and Traugott, E. (2003). *Grammaticalization*. Cambridge University Press, Cambridge. DOI: 10.1017/CBO9781139165525. 22

Huddleston, R. and Pullum, G. K. (2002). *The Cambridge Grammar of the English Language*. Cambridge University Press, Cambridge. 19, 40, 74, 75, 86, 90, 110

Iggesen, O. A. (2011a). Asymmetrical case-marking. In M. S. Dryer and M. Haspelmath, editors, *The World Atlas of Language Structures Online*. Max Planck Digital Library, Munich. 41

Iggesen, O. A. (2011b). Number of cases. In M. S. Dryer and M. Haspelmath, editors, *The World Atlas of Language Structures Online*. Max Planck Digital Library, Munich. 41, 84

Ivanova, A., Oepen, S., Øvrelid, L., and Flickinger, D. (2012). Who did what to whom? A contrastive study of syntacto-semantic dependencies. In *Proceedings of the Sixth Linguistic Annotation Workshop*, pages 2–11, Jeju, Republic of Korea. Association for Computational Linguistics. 81, 88, 109

Jackendoff, R. (1972). *Semantic Interpretation in Generative Grammar*. MIT Press, Cambridge MA. 79

Jespersen, O. (1965). *A Modern English Grammar on Historical Principles, Part VI, Morphology*. George Allen and Unwin Ltd., London. 113

Johnson, C. and Fillmore, C. J. (2000). The FrameNet tagset for frame-semantic and syntactic coding of predicate-argument structure. In *1st Meeting of the North American Chapter of the Association for Computational Linguistics*, pages 56–62. 121

Joppen, S. and Wunderlich, D. (1995). Argument linking in Basque. *Lingua*, **97**(2–3), 123–169. DOI: 10.1016/0024-3841(95)00025-U. 94

Kaplan, R. M. and Bresnan, J. (1982). Lexical-funcational grammar: A formal system for grammatical represenation. In J. Bresnan, editor, *The Mental Representation of Grammatical Relations*, pages 173–281. The MIT Press, Cambridge MA. 80, 81, 124

Karlsson, F. (1983). *Finnish: An Essential Grammar*. Routledge, London. Translated by Andrew Chesterman. 40

Karlsson, F. (1998). *Yleinen Kielitiede [General Linguistics]*. Helsinki. 24, 25

Katamba, F. (2003). Bantu nominal morphology. In D. Nurse and G. Philippson, editors, *The Bantu Languages*, pages 103–120. Routledge, London. 39

Kay, P. (2005). Argument structure constructions and the argument-adjunct distinction. In M. Fried and H. C. Boas, editors, *Grammatical Construstions: Back to the Roots*, pages 71–98. 65, 66

Keenan, E. L. (1976). Towards a universal definition of "subject". In C. N. Li, editor, *Subject and Topic*, pages 303–333. Academic Press, Inc., New York. 83

Keenan, E. L. and Comrie, B. (1977). Noun phrase accessibility and universal grammar. *Linguistic Inquiry*, **8**(1), 63–99. 85

Kegl, J., Coppola, M., and Senghas, A. (1999). Creation through contact: Sign language emergence and sign language change in Nicaragua. In M. DeGraff, editor, *Language Creation and Language Change: Creolization, Diacrhony, and Development*, pages 179–237. MIT Press, Cambridge, MA. 7

Kibort, A. and Corbett, G. G. (2008). Number. In *Grammatical Features*. 38, 51

Kingsbury, P. and Palmer, M. (2002). From treebank to PropBank. In *Proceedings of the 3rd International Confernce on Language Resources and Evaluation (LREC2002)*, Las Palmas, Spain. 74, 77, 80

Kiss, T. (2005). Semantic constraints on relative clause extraposition. *Natural Language and Linguistic Theory*, **23**(2), 281–334. DOI: 10.1007/s11049-003-1838-7. 119

Klausenburger, J. (1984). *French Liaison and Linguistic Theory*. Steiner, Stuttgart. 33

Koptjevskaja-Tamm, M. (2012). *Nominalizations*. Routledge. 46

Kornai, A. and Pullum, G. K. (1990). The X-bar theory of phrase structure. *Language*, **66**(1), 24–50. DOI: 10.1353/lan.1990.0015. 64

Kornfilt, J. (1997). *Turkish*. Routledge, New York. 95, 98, 99, 106

Kozinsky, I., Nedjalkov, V., and Polinskaja, M. (1988). Antipassive in Chukchee. In M. Shibatani, editor, *Passive and Voice*, pages 651–706. John Benjamins, Amsterdam. 103

Labov, W. (1982). Building on empirical foundations. In W. P. Lehmann and M. Yakov, editors, *Perspectives on Historical Linguistics*, pages 17–92. John Benjamins Publishing Company. 22

Lambrecht, K. (1996). *Information Structure and Sentence Form: Topic, Focus, and the Mental Representations of Discourse Referents*. Cambridge University Press, Cambridge, UK. 101, 110

Langacker, R. W. (1995). Possession and possessive constructions. In J. R. Taylor and R. E. MacLaury, editors, *Language and the Cognitive Construal of the World*, pages 51–79. Mouton de Gruyter, Berlin. 45

Lasersohn, P. (1989). On the readings of plural noun phrases. *Linguistic Inquiry*, **20**(1), pp. 130–134. 115

Le Nagard, R. and Koehn, P. (2010). Aiding pronoun translation with co-reference resolution. In *Proceedings of the Joint Fifth Workshop on Statistical Machine Translation and MetricsMATR*, pages 252–261, Uppsala, Sweden. Association for Computational Linguistics. 40

Lehrer, A. (1988). A note on the semantics of -ist and -ism. *American Speech*, **63**(2), 181–185. DOI: 10.2307/454426. 16

Levin, B. (1993). *English Verb Classes and Alternations: A Preliminary Investigation*. University of Chicago Press, Chicago. 67, 99, 104, 105, 106

Lewis, D. (1979). Scorekeeping in a language game. *Journal of Philosophical Language*, **8**, 339–359. DOI: 10.1007/978-3-642-67458-7_12. 43

Lewis, M. P., editor (2009). *Ethnologue: Languages of the World*. SIL International, Dallas, TX, sixteenth edition. Online version: http://www.ethnologue.com. 6, 7, 8

Liu, B., Qian, L., Wang, H., and Zhou, G. (2010). Dependency-driven feature-based learning for extracting protein-protein interactions from biomedical text. In *Coling 2010: Posters*, pages 757–765, Beijing, China. Coling 2010 Organizing Committee. 88

MacDonald, M. C. (1994). Probabilistic constraints and syntactic ambiguity resolution. *Language and Cognitive Processes*, **9**, 157–201. DOI: 10.1080/01690969408402115. 102

Marantz, A. P. (1984). *On the Nature of Grammatical Relations*. Ph.D. thesis, MIT. 80

Marchand, H. (1969). *The Categories and Types of Present-Day English Word-Formation: A Synchronic-Diachronic Approach*. Beck, München, second edition. 19

Marcus, M. P., Santorini, B., and Marcinkiewicz, M. A. (1993). Building a large annotated corpus of English: The Penn Treebank. *Computational Linguistics*, **19**(2), 313–330. 21, 58, 61, 80, 110

Marten, L. (2011). Bemba benefactive construction in the typology of applicatives. In *Proceedings of the 3rd Conference on Language Description and Theory*, pages 183–192, London. SOAS. 99

Maslova, E. (2003). *A Grammar of Kolyma Yukaghir*, volume 27 of *Mouton Grammar Library*. Mouton de Gruyter, Berlin / New York. DOI: 10.1515/9783110197174. 41

Matsumoto, Y., Kitauchi, A., Yamashita, T., and Hirano, Y. (1999). Japanese morphological analysis system ChaSen version 2.0 manual. Technical report, NAIST. NAIST-IS-TR99009. 123

Maynor, N. (1979). The morpheme *un*. *American Speech*, **54**(4), 310–11. DOI: 10.2307/454704. 19

McCloskey, J. (1997). Subjecthood and subject positions. In L. Haegeman, editor, *Elements of Grammar*, pages 197–234. Kluwer Academic Publishers, Dordrecht. 80

McMahon, A. and McMahon, R. (2003). Finding families: Quantitative methods in language classification. *Transactions of the Philological Society*, **101**(1), 7–55. DOI: 10.1111/1467-968X.00108. 8

Meillet, A. (1925). *La méthode comparative en linguistique historique*. ⬚douard Champion, Paris. 6, 7

Meyers, A., Reeves, R., Macleod, C., Szekely, R., Zielinska, V., Young, B., and Grishman, R. (2004). The NomBank project: An interim report. In A. Meyers, editor, *HLT-NAACL 2004 Workshop: Frontiers in Corpus Annotation*, pages 24–31, Boston, Massachusetts, USA. Association for Computational Linguistics. 67

Miller, P. H. (1992). *Clitics and Constituents in Phrase Structure Grammar*. Garland, New York. 20, 21

Mitchell, K. J., Becich, M. J., Berman, J. J., Chapman, W. W., Gilbertson, J., Gupta, D., Harrison, J., Legowski, E., and Crowley, R. S. (2004). Implementation and evaluation of a negation tagger in a pipeline-based system for information extraction from pathology reports. *Medinfo*, **2004**, 663–667. 42

Mithun, M. (1984). The evolution of noun incorporation. *Language*, **60**(4), 847–894. DOI: 10.1353/lan.1984.0038. 16

Mitkov, R. (1998). Robust pronoun resolution with limited knowledge. In *Proceedings of the 36th Annual Meeting of the Association for Computational Linguistics and 17th International Conference on Computational Linguistics, Volume 2*, pages 869–875, Montréal, Canada. Association for Computational Linguistics. DOI: 10.3115/980691.980712. 43

Monachesi, P. (1993). Object clitics and clitic climbing in Italian HPSG grammar. In *Proceedings of the Sixth Conference of the European Chapter of the Association for Computational Linguistics*, pages 437–442. DOI: 10.3115/976744.976796. 20

Moravcsik, E. (1978). Agreement. In J. H. Greenberg, C. A. Ferguson, and E. A. Moravcsik, editors, *Universals of Human Language, Vol 4: Syntax*, pages 331–374. Stanford University Press, Stanford CA. 47

Moschitti, A. and Basili, R. (2005). Verb subcategorization kernels for automatic semantic labeling. In *Proceedings of the ACL-SIGLEX Workshop on Deep Lexical Acquisition*, pages 10–17, Ann Arbor, Michigan. Association for Computational Linguistics. DOI: 10.3115/1631850.1631852. 66

Moseley, C., Asher, R. E., and Tait, M., editors (1994). *Atlas of the World's Languages*. Routledge. 7

Muansuwan, N. (2002). *Verb Complexes in Thai*. Ph.D. thesis, University at Buffalo. 114

Musan, R. (2001). The present perfect in German. *Natural Language & Linguistic Theory*, **19**(2), 355–401. 36

Nakiboglu-Demiralp, M. (2001). The referential properties of implicit arguments of impersonal passive constructions. In E. Erguvanlı Taylan, editor, *The Verb in Turkish*, pages 129–150. John Benjamins, Amsterdam. 104

Ng, V. and Cardie, C. (2002). Identifying anaphoric and non-anaphoric noun phrases to improve coreference resolution. In *Proceedings of the 19th international conference on Computational linguistics-Volume 1*, pages 1–7. Association for Computational Linguistics. DOI: 10.3115/1072228.1072367. 43

Nichols, J. (1986). Head-marking and dependent-marking grammar. *Language*, **62**(1), 56–119. DOI: 10.2307/415601. 97

Nichols, J. (1992). *Linguistic Diversity in Space and Time*. University of Chicago Press, Chicago. DOI: 10.7208/chicago/9780226580593.001.0001. 6

Nichols, J. (2011). *Ingush Grammar*. University of California Press. 4

Nichols, J. and Bickel, B. (2011). Locus of marking in possessive noun phrases. In M. S. Dryer and M. Haspelmath, editors, *The World Atlas of Language Structures Online*. Max Planck Digital Library, Munich. 45

Nicholson, J., Baldwin, T., and Blunsom, P. (2006). Die Morphologie (f): Targeted lexical acquisition for languages other than English. In *Proceedings of the 2006 Australian Language Technology Workshop (ALTW 2006)*, pages 67–74, Sydney, Australia. 50

Noonan, M. (1992). *A Grammar of Lango*. Mouton de Gruyter, Berlin. DOI: 10.1515/9783110850512. 13

Noonan, M. (2007). Complementation. In T. Shopen, editor, *Language Typology and Syntactic Description. Volume II: Complex Constructions*, pages 52–150. Cambridge University Press, Cambridge, second edition. 84

Nordhoff, S., Hammarström, H., and Haspelmath, M. (2011). Langdoc. Leipzig: Max Planck Institute for Evolutionary Anthropology. Online: `http://glottolog.livingsources.org/`. 7

Nordlinger, R. (1998). *A Grammar of Wambaya, Northern Australia*. Research School of Pacific and Asian Studies, The Australian National University, Canberra. 38, 39, 49, 93, 99, 118

Oates, L. F. (1964). *A Tentative Description of the Gunwinggu Language*. University of Sydney, Sydney. 16

Oepen, S., Flickinger, D., Toutanova, K., and Manning, C. D. (2004). LinGO Redwoods. A rich and dynamic treebank for HPSG. *Journal of Research on Language and Computation*, **2**(4), 575–596. DOI: 10.1007/s11168-004-7430-4. 124

Oflazer, K. (1996). Error-tolerant finite-state recognition with applications to morphological analysis and spelling correction. *Computational Linguistics*, **22**(1), 74–89. 24

O'Grady, W., Archibald, J., Aronoff, M., and Rees-Miller, J. (2010). *Contemporary Linguistics: An Introduction*. Bedford/St. Martin's, Boston, sixth edition. 16, 17, 18, 126

Osvaldo, J. A. (1986). Passive. *Linguistic Inquiry*, **17**(4), 587–622. 103, 104

Palmer, F. (2001). *Mood and Modality*. Cambridge University Press, Cambridge. DOI: 10.1017/CBO9781139167178. 36

Palmer, M., Gildea, D., and Kingsbury, P. (2005). The proposition bank: An annotated corpus of semantic roles. *Computational Linguistics*, **31**(1), 71–105. DOI: 10.1162/0891201053630264. 80

Payne, D. L. and Payne, T. (1990). Yagua. In D. C. Derbyshire and G. K. Pullum, editors, *Handbook of Amazonian Languages 2*, pages 249–474. Mouton de Gruyter, Berlin. DOI: 10.1515/9783110860382. 51

Petrov, S., Das, D., and McDonald, R. (2012). A universal part-of-speech tagset. In N. Calzolari, K. Choukri, T. Declerck, M. U. Doğan, B. Maegaard, J. Mariani, J. Odijk, and S. Piperidis, editors, *Proceedings of the Eighth International Conference on Language Resources and Evaluation (LREC-2012)*, pages 2089–2096, Istanbul, Turkey. European Language Resources Association (ELRA). ACL Anthology Identifier: L12-1115. 59, 60

Phillips, B. S. (2001). Lexical diffusion, lexical frequency, and lexical analysis. In J. L. Bybee and P. Hopper, editors, *Frequency and the Emergence of Linguistic Structure*, pages 123–136. John Benjamins Publishing Company. 33

Phillips, C. (2003). Linear order and constituency. *Linguistic Inquiry*, **34**(1), 37–90. DOI: 10.1162/002438903763255922. 63

Polinsky, M. (2011). Antipassive constructions. In M. S. Dryer and M. Haspelmath, editors, *The World Atlas of Language Structures Online*. Max Planck Digital Library, Munich. 103

Pollard, C. and Sag, I. A. (1992). Anaphors in English and the scope of binding theory. *Linguistic Inquiry*, **23**(2), 261–303. 85

Pollard, C. and Sag, I. A. (1994). *Head-Driven Phrase Structure Grammar*. Studies in Contemporary Linguistics. The University of Chicago Press and CSLI Publications, Chicago, IL and Stanford, CA. 64, 124

Postal, P. M. (1964). Underlying and superficial linguistic structure. *Harvard Educational Review*, **34**, 246–266. 53

Poulson, L. (2011). Meta-modeling of tense and aspect in a cross-linguistic grammar engineering platform. In *University of Washington Working Papers in Linguistics*, volume 28. 36

Prince, A. and Smolensky, P. (1993). Optimality Theory: Constraint interaction in generative grammar. Rutgers University and University of Colorado, Boulder. 29

Prince, E. F. (1981). Topicalization, focus-movement, and yiddish-movement: A pragmatic differentiation. In *Proceedings of the Seventh Annual Meeting of the Berkeley Linguistics Society*, pages 249–264. 116

Pullum, G. (2012). Being a noun. *The Chronicle of Higher Education: Blogs*, (June 20, 2012). 58

Pullum, G. K. and Scholz, B. C. (2010). Recursion in human language. In H. van der Hulst, editor, *Recursion in Human Language*, pages 113–138. Mouton de Gruyter, Berlin. 53

Pustejovsky, J. (1991). The generative lexicon. *Computational Linguistics*, **17**(4), 409–441. 65

Rankin, R. L. (2008). The comparative method. In B. D. Joseph and R. D. Janda, editors, *The Handbook of Historical Linguistics*, pages 199–212. Blackwell Publishing Ltd, Malden, MA. 6, 7

Rastrow, A., Khudanpur, S., and Dredze, M. (2012). Revisiting the case for explicit syntactic information in language models. In *Proceedings of the NAACL-HLT 2012 Workshop: Will We Ever Really Replace the N-gram Model? On the Future of Language Modeling for HLT*, pages 50–58, Montréal, Canada. Association for Computational Linguistics. 88

Reddy, M. (1993). The conduit metaphor: A case of frame conflict in our language about language. In A. Ortony, editor, *Metaphor and Thought*, pages 164–201. Cambridge University Press, New York, 2nd edition. DOI: 10.1017/CBO9781139173865. 54

Reichenbach, H. (1947). *Elements of Symbolic Logic*. Free Press, New York. 36

Reynolds, K. H. and Eastman, C. M. (1989). Morphologically based agreement in Swahili. *Studies in African Linguistics*, **20**(1). 46

Rimell, L., Clark, S., and Steedman, M. (2009). Unbounded dependency recovery for parser evaluation. In *Proceedings of the 2009 Conference on Empirical Methods in Natural Language Processing*, pages 813–821, Singapore. Association for Computational Linguistics. 118, 124

Rosenbaum, P. (1967). *The Grammar of English Predicate Complement Constructions*. MIT Press, Cambridge, MA. 110

Ross, J. R. (1967). *Constraints on Variables in Syntax*. Ph.D. thesis, MIT. Published as Infinite Syntax! Norwood, N.J.: Ablex, 1986. 117

Rudin, C. (1988). On multiple questions and multiple WH fronting. *Natural Language and Linguistic Theory*, **6**(4), 445–501. DOI: 10.1007/BF00134489. 117

Ruppenhofer, J., Ellsworth, M., Petruck, M. R. L., Johnson, Christopher, R., and Scheffczyk, J. (2010). *FrameNet II: Extended Theory and Practice*. available from `https://framenet2.icsi.berkeley.edu/docs/r1.5/book.pdf`. 81, 82, 83, 121

Sag, I. A. and Pollard, C. (1991). An integrated theory of complement control. *Language*, **67**, 63–113. DOI: 10.2307/415539. 110

Sag, I. A., Wasow, T., and Bender, E. M. (2003). *Syntactic Theory: A Formal Introduction*. CSLI, Stanford, CA, second edition. 18, 23, 40, 53, 80, 96, 102, 124

Schachter, P. and Shopen, T. (2007). Parts-of-speech systems. In T. Shopen, editor, *Language Typology and Syntactic Description, Vol 1: Clause Structure*, pages 1–60. Cambridge University Press, Cambridge, second edition. 57, 59

Schütze, C. T. (1996). *The Empirical Base of Linguistics: Grammaticality Judgments and Linguistic Methodology*. University of Chicago Press, Chicago. 4

Sekerina, I. A. (1997). *The Syntax and Processing of Scrambling Constructions in Russian*. Ph.D. thesis, The City University of New York. 92

Shen, L., Xu, J., and Weischedel, R. (2010). String-to-dependency statistical machine translation. *Computational Linguistics*, **36**, 649–671. DOI: 10.1162/coli_a_00015. 88

Siewierska, A. (2004). *Person*. Cambridge University Press, Cambridge. DOI: 10.1017/CBO9780511812729. 38

Siewierska, A. (2011a). Alignment of verbal person marking. In M. S. Dryer and M. Haspelmath, editors, *The World Atlas of Language Structures Online*. Max Planck Digital Library, Munich. 94, 96

Siewierska, A. (2011b). Passive constructions. In M. S. Dryer and M. Haspelmath, editors, *The World Atlas of Language Structures Online*. Max Planck Digital Library, Munich. 103

Siewierska, A. (2011c). Verbal person marking. In M. S. Dryer and M. Haspelmath, editors, *The World Atlas of Language Structures Online*. Max Planck Digital Library, Munich. 47, 83, 94

Silverstein, M. (1972). Chinook Jargon: Language contact and the problem of multi-level generative systems, II. *Language*, **48**, 596–625. DOI: 10.2307/412037. 103

Simpson, J. and Withgott, M. (1986). Pronominal clitic clusters and templates. In H. Borer, editor, *Syntax and Semantics 19: The Syntax of Pronominal Clitics*, pages 149–174. Academic Press, New York. 21

Snyder, B. and Barzilay, R. (2008). Unsupervised multilingual learning for morphological segmentation. In *Proceedings of ACL-08: HLT*, pages 737–745, Columbus, Ohio. Association for Computational Linguistics. 123

Soga, M. (1983). *Tense and Aspect in Modern Colloquial Japanese*. University of British Columbia Press. 52

Song, J. J. (2001). *Linguistic Typology: Morphology and Syntax*. Pearson Education., Harlow. 106

Song, J. J. (2011). Nonperiphrastic causative constructions. In M. S. Dryer and M. Haspelmath, editors, *The World Atlas of Language Structures Online*. Max Planck Digital Library, Munich. 106

Starosta, S., Kuiper, K., Ng, S.-A., and Wu, Z.-Q. (1997). On defining the Chinese compound word: Headedness in Chinese compounding and Chinese VR compounds. In J. L. Packard, editor, *New Approaches to Chinese Word Formation*, pages 347–370. Mouton de Gruyter, Berlin. DOI: 10.1515/9783110809084. 15

Stassen, L. (2000). AND-languages and WITH-languages. *Linguistic Typology*, **4**, 1–54. DOI: 10.1515/lity.2000.4.1.1. 115

Stassen, L. (2011). Noun phrase conjunction. In M. S. Dryer and M. Haspelmath, editors, *The World Atlas of Language Structures Online*. Max Planck Digital Library, Munich. 69

Stiebels, B. (2007). Towards a typology of complement control. *ZAS Papers in Linguistics*, **47**, 1–80. 112

Stump, G. (2001). *Inflectional Morphology. A Theory of Paradigm Structure*. Cambridge University Press, Cambridge. DOI: 10.1017/CBO9780511486333. 11

Surdeanu, M., Johansson, R., Meyers, A., Màrquez, L., and Nivre, J. (2008). The CoNLL 2008 shared task on joint parsing of syntactic and semantic dependencies. In *CoNLL 2008: Proceedings of the Twelfth Conference on Computational Natural Language Learning*, pages 159–177, Manchester, England. Coling 2008 Organizing Committee. DOI: 10.3115/1596324.1596352. 88

Szabó, Z. G. (2008). Compositionality. In E. N. Zalta, editor, *The Stanford Encyclopedia of Philosophy*. Winter 2008 edition. 54

Thomason, S. G. and Kaufman, T. (1988). *Language Contact, Creolization, and Genetic Linguistics*. University of California Press, Berkeley, CA. 6, 7

Toutanova, K., Suzuki, H., and Ruopp, A. (2008). Applying morphology generation models to machine translation. In *Proceedings of ACL-08: HLT*, pages 514–522, Columbus, Ohio. Association for Computational Linguistics. 47, 123

Trager, G. L. (1955). French morphology: Verb inflection. *Language*, **31**(4), 511–529. DOI: 10.2307/411364. 31

Tseng, J. (2003). Phrasal affixes and French morphosyntax. In G. Jäger, P. Monachesi, G. Penn, and S. Wintner, editors, *Proceedings of Formal Grammar 2003*, pages 177–188, Stanford. CSLI Publications. 33

Vainikka, A. (1993). The three structural cases in Finnish. In A. Holmberg and U. Nikanne, editors, *Case and Other Functional Categories in Finnish Syntax*, pages 129–159. Mouton de Gruyter, Berlin. 40

van der Auwera, J., Lejeune, L., Pappuswamy, U., and Goussev, V. (2011). The morphological imperative. In M. S. Dryer and M. Haspelmath, editors, *The World Atlas of Language Structures Online*. Max Planck Digital Library, Munich. 46

van Enk, G. J. and de Vries, L. (1997). *The Korowai of Irian Jaya: Their Language in its Cultural Context*. Oxford University Press, Oxford. 43

van Riemsdijk, H. and Williams, E. (1986). *Introduction to the Theory of Grammar*. MIT Press, Cambridge MA. 80

Voegelin, C. F. and Voegelin, F. M. (1977). *Classification and Index of the World's Languages*. Elsevier, New York. 7

Volokh, A. and Neumann, G. (2010). 372:Comparing the benefit of different dependency parsers for textual entailment using syntactic constraints only. In *Proceedings of the 5th International Workshop on Semantic Evaluation*, pages 308–312, Uppsala, Sweden. Association for Computational Linguistics. 88

Wälchli, B. (2012). Indirect measurement in morphological typology. In A. Ender, A. Leemann, and B. Wälchli, editors, *Methods in Contemporary Linguistics*, pages 69–92. de Gruyter, Berlin. DOI: 10.1515/9783110275681. 24, 25

Wiegand, M., Balahur, A., Roth, B., Klakow, D., and Montoyo, A. (2010). A survey on the role of negation in sentiment analysis. In *Proceedings of the Workshop on Negation and Speculation in Natural Language Processing*, pages 60–68, Uppsala, Sweden. University of Antwerp. 42

Wierzbicka, A. (2000). Lexical prototypes as a universal basic for cross-linguistic identification of "parts of speech". In P. M. Vogel and B. Comrie, editors, *Approaches to the Typology of Word Classes*, pages 285–318. Mouton de Gruyter, Berlin. 58

Xue, N. (2001). *Defining and Automatically Identifying Words in Chinese*. Ph.D. thesis, University of Delaware. 20

Yamaji, H. (2000). Addressee-oriented nature of referent honorfics in Japanese conversation. In *Proceedings of the Eigth Annual Symposium about Language and Society*. 44

Zaenen, A. and Crouch, D. (2009). OBLs hobble computations. In M. Butt and T. H. King, editors, *Proceedings of LFG09*, pages 644–654. CSLI Publications. 81

Zaenen, A., Maling, J., and Thráinsson, H. (1985). Case and grammatical functions: The Icelandic passive. *NLLT*, **3**(4), 441–483. DOI: 10.1007/BF00133285. 84

Zhang, Y. and Kordoni, V. (2006). Automated deep lexical acquisition for robust open texts processing. In *Proceedings of the Fifth International Conference on Language Resources and Evaluation (LREC 2006)*, pages 275–280. 66

Zwicky, A. M. (1982). Stranded *to* and phonological phrasing in English. *Linguistics*, **20**, 3–57. DOI: 10.1515/ling.1982.20.1-2.3. 23

Zwicky, A. M. (1985a). Clitics and particles. *Language*, **61**(2), 283–305. DOI: 10.2307/414146. 59

Zwicky, A. M. (1985b). Heads. *Journal of Linguistics*, **21**(1), 1–29. DOI: 10.1017/S0022226700010008. 65

Zwicky, A. M. and Pullum, G. K. (1983). Cliticization vs. inflection: English *n't*. *Language*, **59**, 502–13. DOI: 10.2307/413900. 18, 21

Author's Biography

EMILY M. BENDER

Emily M. Bender is an Associate Professor in the Department of Linguistics and Adjunct Associate Professor in the Department of Computer Science & Engineering at the University of Washington. Her primary research interests lie in multilingual grammar engineering and the incorporation of linguistic knowledge, especially from linguistic typology, in NLP. She is the PI of the Grammar Matrix project, which is developed in the context of the DELPH-IN Consortium (Deep Linguistic Processing with HPSG Initiative). More generally, she is interested in the intersection of linguistics and computational linguistics, from both directions: bringing computational methodologies to linguistic science and linguistic science to natural language processing.

Her PhD (in linguistics) is from Stanford University. She has authored or co-authored papers in *Linguistic Issues in Language Technology,* the *Journal of Research on Language and Computation, English Language and Linguistics,* the *Encyclopedia of Language and Linguistics,* and the proceedings of ACL, COLING, IJCNLP, and associated workshops.

General Index

Index of Languages

Made in United States
North Haven, CT
24 November 2021

11477067R00102